THE GENESIS FACTOR

THE GENESIS FACTOR

PROBING
LIFE'S
BIG
QUESTIONS

DAVID R. HELM
JON M. DENNIS

CROSSWAY BOOKS • WHEATON, ILLINOIS
A DIVISION OF GOOD NEWS PUBLISHERS

The Genesis Factor

Published by Crossway Books
   a division of Good News Publishers
   1300 Crescent Street
   Wheaton, Illinois 60187

Cover design: David LaPlaca

Cover photo: The Image Bank & PhotoDisc™

Author photo: Randall Gruendyke

First printing, 2001

Printed in the United States of America

Unless otherwise noted, all Bible quotations are taken from *Holy Bible: New International Version,* copyright © 1978 by the New York International Bible Society. Used by permission of Zondervan Bible Publishers.

Library of Congress Cataloging-in-Publication Data
Helm, David R., 1961–
 The Genesis factor : probing life's big questions / David R. Helm,
Jon M. Dennis.
  p. cm.
 Includes bibliographical references.
 ISBN 1-58134-285-3 (pbk. : alk. paper)
 1. Bible O. T. Genesis I-III—Criticism, interpretation, etc. 2. Bible—
Evidences, authority, etc. 3. Apologetics. I. Dennis, Jon M., 1966–
II. Title.
BS1235.52 . H45 2001
239—dc21   2001001915
                 CIP

15	14	13	12	11	10	09	08	07	06	05	04	03	02	01
15	14	13	12	11	10	9	8	7	6	5	4	3	2	1

TABLE OF CONTENTS

PREFACE

This book is for people who have a healthy uncertainty about life's big questions—who, while knowing many things, reserve a measure of doubt on most everything.

Levin, a character in Tolstoy's *Anna Karenina*, gives voice to such doubt during his confession to a priest:

> "I have doubted everything, and I still do," Levin replied in a voice he himself found unpleasant, and fell silent.
>
> The priest waited a few seconds to see whether he was going to say something else, then closed his eyes and said quickly, in a provincial accent:
>
> "Doubts are natural to human weakness, but we must pray, that we may be strengthened by divine compassion. What in particular are your sins?" he added without the slightest interval, as though trying not to lose time.
>
> "My principal sin is doubt. I doubt everything, and I am in doubt most of the time."
>
> "Doubt is natural to human weakness," the priest said, repeating the same words. "But what do you doubt most of all?"
>
> "I doubt everything. Sometimes I doubt even the existence of God," said Levin involuntarily, and was horrified at the indecency of what he had said. But Levin's words seemed to make no impression on the priest.[1]

Levin desired an intellectual exchange with the priest. He wanted to probe and explore life's big questions. Unfortunately, the priest never entered into conversation. For him, doubt was a sign of human weakness to be overcome by unquestioned acquiescence to the traditions of the church.

The purpose of this book is to have a conversation with the Levins of our day, those who are unsure what to make of the Christian faith. And while we, the authors, are Christians, we have no illusions about deciding life's big questions for anyone. Renowned New Testament scholar J. Gresham Machen, in introducing one of his own books, captures our sentiment:

> The purpose of this book is not to decide the religious issue of the present day, but merely to present the issue as sharply and clearly as possible, in order that the reader may be aided in deciding for himself.[2]

We write in the spirit of C. S. Lewis, who in the preface to *Mere Christianity* said:

> In this book I am not trying to convert anyone to my own position. Ever since I became a Christian I have thought that the best, perhaps the only, service I could do for my unbelieving neighbors was to explain and defend the belief that has been common to nearly all Christians at all times.[3]

This is the desire behind *The Genesis Factor*. It is an invitation to examine some important issues. It is a request for the reader to consider the ultimate questions of life where Christianity begins — with the book of beginnings.

— David Helm and Jon Dennis
Chicago, 2001

In the beginning God created the heavens and the earth.

—GENESIS 1:1

1

A CONVERSATION
STARTER

Most of us have heard people asking life's big questions. Such questions are timeless. They confront every living person and contemplate the greatest of themes. They unite us to all peoples of the past as well as to those who will follow.

They are questions such as:

> *Is there a God? And, if so, does this God (he, she, or it) care about what is going on down here?*
> *Where did everything come from?*
> *Is the meaning in the universe?*
> *Who are we, really?*
> *Where did evil come from?*
> *What is the matter with people?*
> *Why can't we fix all our problems?*
> *Is there any hope for the human race?*

In today's individualized way of viewing the world, some of these questions become personal: "Who am I?" "Where did I come from?" "Where am I going?" And, "Is there any divinely orchestrated meaning to my life?"

Many people today are eager to find answers to these big questions. The sales of Stephen Hawking's book *A Brief History of Time* attest to this interest. The book was on the *London Sunday Times* bestseller list for 237 weeks, has been translated into forty languages, and has sold one copy for every 750 people in the world.[1]

Concerning its popularity, Hawking writes,

> The success of *A Brief History* indicates that there is widespread interest in the big questions like: Where did I come from? And why is the universe the way it is?[2]

And doesn't this "widespread interest in the big questions" make sense? After all, if we are to live with a proper sense of being human then shouldn't we, at some point in our lives, pursue these questions? And if so, what intellectual traditions should guide our exploration? What voices should we be interacting with? Ideally, probing life's big questions together would take place face-to-face around a table — in a local restaurant, perhaps, over a leisurely meal. There are already a host of voices at the table — people who are willing to interact with us.

SOME VOICES AT THE TABLE

There is, for instance, the voice of *naturalism:* "Why all the talk about where we came from, or if there is a god? I believe what Carl Sagan said: 'The cosmos is all there is, or has been, or will be.'"[3]

Naturalism will be a familiar voice for most of our readers. Naturalism holds that matter is the essence of reality. Some label this view "philosophical materialism."

Naturalism, while clearly belonging at the table, may have some self-imposed limitations when it comes to the bigger questions of life. By design, it limits itself to that which can be externally verified. In the words of a *Time* magazine article on religion and science, "Science was for the real world: machines, manufactured things, medicines, guns, moon rockets. Religion was for everything else."[4]

Lesslie Newbigin, in his perceptive book *Foolishness to the Greeks*, outlines how naturalism tends to relegate life's big questions to the periphery. He argues that naturalism is limited to a closed system. It deals only in the world of facts and data; it is concerned with physics, not metaphysics; *real* things, not *spiritual* things.[5]

What is good about naturalism is its impetus to exploration. At the same time, however, some people, while quite comfortable with naturalism, are uneasy with some of its implications. They feel something is missing in a world without God. Contemporary theologian David Wells describes the rise of this new voice for us. It is the voice of *pervasive supernaturalism*:

> [T]he world, so recently emptied of the divine, is now awash with the supernatural intrusions, with strange voices and mystical experiences of every conceivable kind. . . . [I]f modernization has robbed our culture of the divine, it has in doing so also sown the seeds of longing for some inner sense of the supernatural.[6]

J. D. Salinger captures this voice poignantly in his short story "Teddy." He describes an incident where a spiritually precocious youngster recalls how he arrived at his view of God while watching his little sister drink her milk: " . . . all of a sudden I saw that she was God and the milk was God. I mean, all she was doing was pouring God into God."[7]

Shirley MacLaine is an advocate of this voice as well. "For you see," she says, "each soul is its own god. You must never worship anyone or anything other than self. For *you* are god."[8]

Pervasive supernaturalism is the view that the universe is to be identified with God. God and nature are thought of as the same reality.[9] New and popular expressions of this voice crop up everywhere today, especially in bookstores. You can't miss the resurgence of interest in Eastern religions, mysticism, the New Age, spiritism, and the occult.

This zealous discovery of God in various places offers a rising sense of self to replace the fading notion of God. It leads some to declare that all things are really the same thing, and, therefore, all things are really God.

Alvin Plantinga, a philosopher at the University of Notre Dame, emphasizes the imaginative and creative aspect of this voice:

> Here the fundamental idea — in sharp contrast to naturalism — is that we human beings, in some deep and important way, are ourselves responsible for the structure and nature of the world; it is we, fundamentally, who are the architects of the universe.[10]

That said, there are still other intellectual traditions vying for an opportunity to guide us in our exploration of life's big questions. One such voice values the contribution of naturalism and is intrigued by the optimism of pervasive supernaturalism, yet wonders if there isn't another way to address life's big questions:

"What about *destiny*? What if life does have some ineffable or transcendant meaning to it?" The voice of destiny is imbedded in the movie *You've Got Mail*, with Tom Hanks and Meg Ryan. From the outset, this movie is one of those guy-meets-girl things. What makes it work for some is watching the relationship come together in ways that neither of them has control over. For believers in destiny, life is controlled by fate.

At this point, some readers might be growing uneasy not only with the number of voices willing to guide us through life's big questions, but with the certitude of their answers. After all, most of us don't line up easily or consistently behind any single voice or intellectual tradition. Rather, we prefer to hold on to a measure of *doubt* about life's big questions. Leo Strauss, who taught at the University of Chicago, expressed a life-long commitment to doubt with these words on the question of God's existence:

> Many of our contemporaries assume tacitly or even explicitly that we know that God as an omnipotent being does not exist. I believe that they are wrong; for how could we know that God as an omnipotent being does not exist? . . . I believe [it is] equally true that human reason cannot establish the existence of God. . . . From this it follows that . . . we are reduced to a state of doubt in regard to the most important question.[11]

Do you see what Strauss is saying? Life's big questions demand a little reverence. He doesn't want us to demean the majesty of the questions. A life-long position of doubt may be the most honest way to go.

And so we've come full circle in our search for guides, all the way back to Levin's doubt. In a short time, a number of widely divergent viewpoints have been expressed. From Stephen Hawking to Carl Sagan, from Salinger and MacLaine to *You've Got Mail* and Leo Strauss, everyone has an opinion about the universal questions that confront us.[12]

THE VOICE OF GENESIS

With this book we hope to add another voice to the list of those who might aid us in our search for answers—the voice of Genesis. Ordinarily today, people don't turn to Genesis in their exploration of life's big questions. After all, its voice speaks so definitively that it seems to chase all doubt away. It can appear to stifle our desire to probe life's big questions. And yet, if we are intellectually honest, the voice of Genesis should at least be given a hearing. While it may not be the only perspective on life's big questions, it is one at least worth some exploration. For centuries people have recognized that Genesis presents us with some very large answers to life's universal questions. Doesn't it make sense to try to listen to its voice—to hear the answers it proposes? Then you can come to your own conclusions about the integrity of its claims.

Some readers may be thinking, *Are you kidding? People haven't taken that book seriously for ages. What could it possibly contribute to our discussion of universal questions?*

But we're not kidding.

We believe Genesis has a great contribution to make to the universal conversation on life's big questions. In fact, we believe it does so clearly—even strikingly—in its opening verse. When Genesis says,

In the beginning *God* . . .

it appears to touch on at least one of life's big questions, namely, the existence of God. The Bible simply advances a declaration of God's existence. By the fourth word in the English text, the presence of God is assumed.

The voice of naturalism might respond, "Are you advocating that we abandon hundreds of years of scientific learning and substitute in its place the voice of Genesis?"

And we would reply, no, not at all. The hostility between Genesis and naturalism has led some people (wrongly so, in our opinion) to discredit scientific pursuits.

Thomas Torrance, the renowned Scottish physicist and theologian, shows us a proper relationship between science and theology: "Theology motivates and gives meaning to science—

science sharpens and clarifies theology."[13] Hopefully, as our conversation with Genesis continues, we will come to a fuller appreciation of Torrance's insight.

On an initial reading, the opening verse of Genesis might also have implications for pervasive supernaturalism:

> In the beginning God *created* . . .

Could the additional word "created" be worth listening to? Isn't it at least plausible to think that there is a distinction between God and the rest of creation? The opening line of Genesis states that "In the beginning God created." You see, we might be in for a lively discussion, because Salinger's milky character sees God in everything, and the voice of Genesis may not see God in that way.

What about destiny? Could Genesis have anything to say to believers in fate?

> In the beginning God created *the heavens and the earth* . . .

The final phrase of Genesis 1:1 claims not only that God exists — and not only that this God creates — but that this God is responsible for having created the totality of the universe. If this were true, then would it not be plausible that God created everything for a purpose? Perhaps there is meaning in the universe. What if Genesis wants us to *know* something about God, ourselves, and our ultimate destiny? What if Genesis could challenge Strauss-like doubt and yet maintain a certain reverence for the questions themselves?

To this point we have only raised areas of interaction as a conversation starter. All we can say thus far is that Genesis might help us explore life's big questions. This has been only a surface reading. We have not yet explored whether the voice of

Genesis can sustain thoughtful and reflectiv-e engagement with the myriad voices vying for our attention. We (the authors) think that the following chapters will show that it can. And we attribute that to what we call "the Genesis factor" — the viable but often overlooked voice for our time.

And so, with the conversation started, we must now leave this exchange and step into the yet starless night of Genesis.

¹In the beginning God created the heavens and the earth. ²Now the earth was formless and empty, darkness was over the surface of the deep, and the Spirit of God was hovering over the waters.

—GENESIS 1:1-2

2

A VIEW OF THE STARS

Anyone reading Genesis seeking answers to life's big questions also brings to the text a set of their own more particular questions—questions such as, "Where are the dinosaurs?" "How long are these creation-days?" "How old is the earth?" Or, "How does this square with macro-evolution?"[1]

But we would ask the reader to set aside these particular questions for a time. As Mortimer Adler has ably pointed out in *How to Read a Book,* the order of the questions we ask of a book are very important. The question, "What is the book about as a whole?" must precede the question, "Is the book true?"[2] This is a fundamental rule of reading: *A book must be understood on its own terms before it can be evaluated.*

That is our goal: to read Genesis on its own terms. No reader can do this perfectly, but with this goal in mind, let's proceed.[3]

GENESIS IS ABOUT GOD

We would argue that Genesis is not so much about dinosaurs, literal days, the age of the earth, or macro-evolution. Certainly people turn to it for these subjects and a host of others. Yet we have come to believe and would suggest that, first and foremost, Genesis is about God. No reading of the text can overlook this fact. It begins with God creating the universe, and it ends with a promise that God will rescue Israel from slavery. And continually in between we find the activity of God. God speaks. God blesses. God banishes. God judges. God chooses. God leads. God delivers. God is to be worshiped. If asked, "What is Genesis about as a whole?" we would reply that, generally speaking, Genesis is about God.

While it should not be overlooked that Genesis at the very least is about God, one can be more specific. We think it can be argued, more specifically, that Genesis is about God's plan to rescue his people through the seed of Abraham.

The writer of Genesis is telling the Israelites where *they* came from (creation) and where *they* are going (redemption). The book of Genesis teaches that Israel's God — the God of Abraham, Isaac, and Jacob — is not a tribal god but is the Lord of the heavens and the earth, and that Israel's God intends to bless all the families of the earth through the seed of Abraham.

No wonder the writer moves so rapidly through primeval history — a mere eleven chapters, spanning thousands of years. No wonder he spends so much more time tracing Israel's *family* history — chapters 12 through 50, covering only five hundred years.

That said, it is still a bit too early in this conversation to answer a subsequent question raised by Adler: "Is the book true"? But for the present, we can say the whole of Genesis is about God.

GENESIS ONE IS ABOUT GOD

If we are right in stating that Genesis at the very least is about God, it should come as no surprise that chapter 1 is also about God. In chapter 1 God is the main character, the key player, the protagonist. Open a Bible and let your eye scan the chapter —

- "In the beginning *God* . . ." (v. 1)

- "And the spirit of *God* was hovering over the waters." (v. 2)

- "And *God* said . . ." (v. 3)

- "And *God* said . . ." (v. 9)

- "And *God* . . ." (v. 14)

- "And *God* . . ." (v. 20)

- "And *God* . . ." (v. 24)

- "Then *God* . . ." (v. 26)

- "So *God* . . ." (v. 27)

God is mentioned thirty-two times in this chapter—God said, God saw, God separated, God called, God made, God set, God created. God.

Now, the assumption that God exists may be difficult for us to swallow. Certain voices may cry out against it. But there is little use arguing that this chapter assumes anything less. It cannot be overlooked that the writer of Genesis writes as if God exists.

So if we ask, "What is Genesis 1 about?" on the simplest level we must say: *God.* What shines forth is the *person* of God. Take a look:

- Chapter 1 presents a *particular* God—the God who created the heavens and the earth—not an abstract idea or a philosophical concept.

• Next, this God is a *preexistent* God. This God precedes the heavens and the earth.[4]

• This is also a *powerful* God. By the power of *words* this God brings things into being. "And God said, 'Let there be light,' and there was light." God speaks, and it is!

• Finally, this a *personal* God. The God of Genesis 1 has a voice and uses words. Each day in the account begins with the phrase, "And God said . . ." What a curious craftsman this God is. Instead of rolling up his sleeves and going to work, this God clears his throat and speaks.

SOME IMPLICATIONS

If we spend our time answering our own particular questions of the text, we could, at the end of the day, miss the overarching point of the text. And that is precisely what some are tempted to do.

This is apparently what happens to Richard Dawkins, the brilliant Oxford defender of evolution. He is so concerned with the question of origins that he overlooks how central God is to Genesis 1:

> Nearly all peoples have their own creation myths, and the Genesis story is just the one that happened to have been adopted by one particular tribe of Middle Eastern herders. It has no more special status than the belief of a particular West African tribe that the world was created from the excrement of ants.[5]

What Dawkins does with Genesis 1 exemplifies our own tendencies when we approach the text. He comes to the text with questions of contemporary relevance foremost in his mind. He wants to determine if Genesis 1 squares with evolution. Further, he displays only a partial interest in the text as a whole by ignoring the relationship of Genesis 1 to the rest of the book. And he intentionally downplays the special status of Genesis as a historical record. The end result is that in Dawkins's mind, God is only supplied as an explanation of how the world came into being and is as secondary as the excrement of ants. He reads only by the lamp of naturalism.

Søren Kierkegaard tells a parable that wonderfully demonstrates how reading only by the light of naturalism keeps one from seeing God:

> When the prosperous man on a dark but starlit night drives comfortably in his carriage and has the lanterns lighted, aye, then he is safe, he fears no difficulty, he carries his light with him, and it is not dark close around him. But precisely because he has the lanterns lighted, and has a strong light close to him, precisely for this reason, he cannot see the stars. For his lights obscure the stars, which the poor peasant, driving without lights, can see gloriously in the dark but starry night. So those deceived ones live in the temporal existence: either, occupied with the necessities of life, they are too busy to avail themselves of the view, or in the prosperity and good days they have, as it were, lanterns lighted, and close about them everything is so satisfactory, so pleasant, so comfortable — but the view is lacking, the prospect, the view of the stars.[6]

Are we too busy to avail ourselves of the view of the stars? Might the light of the particular questions that we naturally bring to the text, in the end, lead us to overlook perhaps the largest of questions that Genesis seems concerned to speak about: "Is there a God?" What we find is, surprisingly, Genesis has its own agenda. And it may not be ours. On the question of God's existence, the voice of Genesis is steady: God exists.

3And God said, "Let there be light," and there was light. 4God saw that the light was good, and he separated the light from the darkness. 5God called the light "day," and the darkness he called "night." And there was evening, and there was morning – the first day.

6And God said, "Let there be an expanse between the waters to separate water from water." 7So God made the expanse and separated the water under the expanse from the water above it. And it was so. 8God called the expanse "sky." And there was evening, and there was morning – the second day.

9And God said, "Let the water under the sky be gathered to one place, and let dry ground appear." And it was so. 10God called the dry ground "land," and the gathered waters he called "seas." And God saw that it was good.

11Then God said, "Let the land produce vegetation: seed-bearing plants and trees on the land that bear fruit with seed in it, according to their various kinds." And it was so. 12The land produced vegetation: plants bearing seed according to their kinds and trees bearing fruit with seed in it according to their kinds. And God saw that it was good. 13And there was evening, and there was morning – the third day.

14And God said, "Let there be lights in the expanse of the sky to separate the day from the night, and let them serve as signs to mark seasons and days and years, 15and let them be lights in the expanse of the sky to give light on the earth." And it was so. 16God made two great lights – the greater light to govern the day and the lesser light to govern the night. He also made the stars. 17God set them in the expanse of the sky to give light on the earth, 18to govern the day and the night, and to separate light from darkness. And God saw that it was good. 19And there was evening, and there was morning – the fourth day.

20And God said, "Let the water teem with living creatures, and let birds fly above the earth across the expanse of the sky." 21So God created the great creatures of the sea and every living and moving thing with which the water teems, according to their kinds, and every winged bird according to its kind. And God saw that it was good. ²²*God blessed them and said, "Be fruitful and increase in number and fill the water in the seas, and let the birds increase on the earth."* ²³*And there was evening, and there was morning – the fifth day.*

²⁴*And God said, "Let the land produce living creatures according to their kinds: livestock, creatures that move along the ground, and wild animals, each according to its kind." And it was so.* ²⁵*God made the wild animals according to their kinds, the livestock according to their kinds, and all the creatures that move along the ground according to their kinds. And God saw that it was good.*

²⁶*Then God said, "Let us make man in our image, in our likeness, and let them rule over the fish of the sea and the birds of the air, over the livestock, over all the earth, and over all the creatures that move along the ground."*

> ²⁷*So God created man in his own image,*
> *in the image of God he created him;*
> *male and female he created them.*

²⁸*God blessed them and said to them, "Be fruitful and increase in number; fill the earth and subdue it. Rule over the fish of the sea and the birds of the air and over every living creature that moves on the ground."*

²⁹*Then God said, "I give you every seed-bearing plant on the face of the whole earth and every tree that has fruit with seed in it. They will be yours for food.* ³⁰*And to all the beasts of the earth and all the birds of the air and all the creatures that move on the ground – everything that has the breath of life in it – I give every green plant for food." And it was so.*

³¹*God saw all that he had made, and it was very good. And there was evening, and there was morning – the sixth day.*

¹*Thus the heavens and the earth were completed in all their vast array.*

—GENESIS 1:3-2:1

3

THE SIX-DAY SONG

N ow, it is one thing for the reader to consider the possibility that God exists. It is quite another to firmly believe that God not only exists, but that he created all things and created them in seven days. Is this what the opening chapter of Genesis teaches? Having been reminded in the last chapter how prone we are to miss the main subject of Genesis 1, we should acknowledge that perhaps we've also missed what Genesis wants to say about how everything came into being. Is Genesis 1 advocating a scientific explanation of the process of creation, or is it putting forward a literary description?

There is a beautiful passage in a children's story that describes the process of creation. A great lion, Aslan, is standing poised to create the universe. His coat is shining and radiant. His mouth is wide open in song, and as he sings, the color green begins to form around his feet and spreads out in a pool. Then flowers and heather appear on the hillside and move out before him. As the tempo of the music picks up, showers of birds fly out of a tree, and butterflies begin to flit about. Finally, the singing becomes wild and frenetic, signaling a great celebration. Aslan says, "Awake. Love. Think. Speak. Be walking trees. Be talking beasts. Be divine waters."[1]

The creation of the world set to music—it is hard to imagine a better metaphor for God's creative work in Genesis 1. Reading the first chapter of the Bible is, in a way, like listening to a symphony. There is the sense of a majestic *forming* and an intricate *filling* among the various movements.

FORMING AND FILLING: GENERAL ARRANGEMENT

One of the endearing qualities of Genesis 1, from a literary standpoint, is its arrangement. It is succinct and orderly. Even a child can follow its melodic line:

- Days 1–3 are creative movements of *forming.*

- Days 4–6 are creative movements of *filling.*

- Day 7 is the cessation of any creative movement.

The general arrangement of the six days of creation divides into two main activities — *forming* and *filling.* Interestingly, the creative movements of forming and filling (which begin in verse 3) both take their cue from the language of verse 2:

Now the earth was *formless and empty* . . . [2]

The earth, which was *formless* at the outset of creation, is given *form* on days 1–3. And the earth, which was *empty* or void at the first stroke of creation, is *filled* on days 4–6.

FORMING AND FILLING: PARTICULAR CORRESPONDENCE

Beyond this general arrangement of the days, however, there is also a *particular correspondence* between the days.

Perhaps an illustration from childhood will help you grasp this notion of correspondence. Do you remember coloring books in which you drew a picture by connecting dots one after another? Well, something like that is going on in Genesis 1. The writer is using the days as dots, so to speak, to fill in a picture that tells us about God's creative activity. Each subsequent day of God's forming and filling activity is related. For instance, there is a particular correspondence or connection between days 1 and 4. On day 1 we learn about light and darkness, day and night. Then, on day 4 we are introduced to the sun and the moon and the stars, which fill up the sky. If we keep connecting, we will see a similar correspondence between days 2 and 5 and also between days 3 and 6. The writer wants us to trace the overall picture of God's creative activity, and he uses correspondence to ensure that we will.[3] He wants us to know that on days 1–3 God *formed* all the places in the universe, and then on days 4–6 he *filled* those places with various creations that would rule over what he had formed.

In our conversation with Genesis to this point we have seen some of the literary beauty of chapter 1. The writer unfolds creation according to a *forming* and a *filling*. Such an intricate pattern will be new to many in our conversation, even those who have been brought up hearing the voice of Genesis.

SOME IMPLICATIONS FOR THE TRADITION OF BIBLICAL LITERALISM

Many today in conservative Christian circles are convinced that the days of Genesis must be literal twenty-four-hour days. This approach to Scripture is, one could argue, a "tradition" in its own right—we could call it "biblical literalism."

Adherents of this school of interpretation see the "days" of Genesis 1 as seven literal twenty-four-hour days, and they often, with the Irish archbishop James Ussher (1581–1656), calculate the age of the earth to be no less than six thousand years and no more than ten thousand years.[4] For the biblical literalist, this is the plain meaning of the text. Adherents to this view find no reason to read it in any way other than literally. For them the conclusions of science regarding the age of the earth must be erroneous, since those conclusions contradict the literal interpretation of the text.

This view is what most of the media and even the general public think of today when using the term "creationism." Many would dread being called a creationist with this understanding of the word. However, creationism in the truest biblical sense does not require that we bind the verses of Genesis 1 in so literal a straitjacket. In actual fact, a creationist is anyone who associates God or a Supreme Being with the origin of the universe. It is possible to hold the view that God created the universe, but without the added baggage of the tenets of creation*ism.*

The most serious difficulty for those who advocate the tradition of biblical literalism will be dealt with in the following chapter, for there we will hear the voice of Genesis use the word "day" without such restricted meaning.

But for now, let every tradition stand back and absorb the aesthetic beauty and goodness of the account itself. The creation account of Genesis 1 is good literature, not a scientific manual. Perhaps a simple but wonderful observation from Sherlock Holmes might help us to step back and appreciate the beauty of our text:

> Our highest assurance of the goodness of providence seems to me to rest in the flowers. All other things, our powers, our desires, our food, are really necessary for our existence in the first instance. But this rose is an extra. Its smell and its color are an embellishment of life not a condition of it. It is only goodness which gives extras and so I say again, that we have much to hope from the flowers.[5]

The details of the creation account are necessary for the existence of the world. But the beauty of the presentation of the text is an extra. We wonder if the color and aesthetic care of the textual arrangement ought not to give us hope — hope that perhaps this text comes from the goodness of Providence. Whatever you think of how historical the text is, take a moment to appreciate the ornate text that has been handed down to us.

The *process* of creation has a certain aesthetic beauty.

THE PINNACLE OF CREATION

The movements of Genesis 1 climax with the creation of mankind. The whole *process* moves toward people as the *pinnacle* of God's creative activity.

Recently, one of us was in conversation with a medical doctor. We were talking about Charles Darwin's *The Origin of Species,* about natural selection and the survival of the fittest. The doctor jokingly pointed out that on a scale of strict quantity, the pinnacle of living things is bacteria, the most tenacious and widely spread class of living organisms. Nice thought, isn't it — bacteria as the pinnacle of creation!

In Genesis 1 it is *mankind* that God crowns as the pinnacle of his creative work. It is for man, male and female, that God shapes, forms, and fills the earth. According to Genesis 1:26-27, God crowns his creation with a very special creature:

> Then God said, "Let us make man in our image, in our likeness, and let them rule over the fish of the sea and the birds of the air, over the livestock, over all the earth, and over all the creatures that move along the ground."
> So God created man in his own image, in the image of God he created him; male and female he created them.

Mankind, then, is distinguished from all of the rest of creation. Men and women are unique because we are created to rule over the rest of God's world. Like a monarch of ancient days who established vassal kings in the far-flung reaches of his empire in order to show his power, God sets us up as "vice-regents" beneath himself to rule over all of creation. Verse 28 confirms this interpretation:

> God blessed them and said to them, "Be fruitful and increase in number; fill the earth and subdue it. Rule over the fish of the sea and the birds of the air and over every living creature that moves on the ground."

Mankind's rule over creation should come as no surprise to the reader. The entire chapter has been filled with God's activity of appointing rulers over his creation. Remember that the creations of days 4–6 were expressly meant to rule over the forms of days 1–3. And mankind is meant to rule over it all.

As you probably have noticed, we have said nothing to this point about day 7. As we will see in the next chapter, while mankind may be the pinnacle of creation, God's rest (on day 7) stands as the climax of the Genesis prologue.

FINAL THOUGHTS

By the end of six days, all of God's creative activity is completed. And it is very good. Everything is working as God intended. The glory of the vast array of God's creation swells beneath the heavens like an immense symphony.

The *person* of creation — the Creator — stands forth as the great subject (as we saw in chapter 2). The *process* of creation heralds a majestic unity. And as the *pinnacle* of creation, mankind is beckoned to carry out God's kingly intentions.

²By the seventh day God had finished the work he had been doing; so on the seventh day he rested from all his work. ³And God blessed the seventh day and made it holy, because on it he rested from all the work of creating that he had done.

4

THE SURPRISE OF SEVEN

I n attempting to listen to Genesis on its own terms, we are discovering that it does interact with life's big questions. Genesis has something to suggest to us about whether or not God exists. It also invites us to consider the presence of a Creator behind the origin of the universe. And as we listen to its voice in this chapter, we will hear that the six days of God's creative activity have a divinely intended goal and meaning.

Of course, many today would doubt such an assumption. Aldous Huxley, the well-known agnostic, once confessed:

> Is the universe possessed of value and meaning? I took for granted that there was no meaning. I had motives for not wanting the world to have a meaning.[1]

Huxley asked, "Is the universe possessed of value and meaning?" We think day 7 may provide a surprising answer. For on that day something significant has *ended,* and something else of greater meaning has *begun.*

GOD'S REST: THE END OF HIS CREATIVE ACTIVITY

According to Genesis 2:2, on day 7 God *rests:*

> So on the seventh day he rested from all his work.

Puzzling isn't it, this idea of a resting God? What can it

mean? Was God tired? No, there is no sign of weariness here. To create the world out of nothing in six days is quite an accomplishment.[2] However, God's voice is not hoarse, his hands are not sore.[3]

Rather, it appears from Genesis 2:2 that God rested because his work of creation was done:

> Thus the heavens and earth were *completed* in all their vast array. (v. 1)

> By the seventh day God *had finished* the work he had been doing. (v. 2)

God's work is done. Every star has been hung. Every proton, neutron, and electron is in place. Gravity itself is up and running. The earth, turning on its axis, follows its orbit around the sun. On the earth, every leaf is attached. Every gill is secure. Every wing is poised for flight. The world, indeed the universe, is complete, fine-tuned in every detail. The reason God rests is because his creative work is done.

The Hebrew word choice confirms the idea that God rests from his creative work. The Hebrew word for "rest" is literally "cease." It comes from the same root as the word for Sabbath — that is, the root word gives rise to both "Sabbath" and "cease" or "rest." In the context of Genesis 2:2-3, God *ceases* from what he has been doing. For six days he has been creating the heavens and the earth, but on the seventh day he stops creating.

Now, this idea of a resting God raises important questions in regard to whether the universe had any divinely intended meaning and purpose: Does God's rest indicate something negative about God? Is God now disengaged from the universe? Is Genesis 2:2-3 teaching us that God has stopped interacting with the entire created order, humanity included? Are we now set adrift to chart our own course and our own sense of meaning in life?

We would argue that the voice of Genesis suggests otherwise. After all, from chapter 3 all the way through the end of the book God continues to interact with humanity. What, then, does God's rest imply? And what does this rest teach us about big questions of meaning and purpose? We shall see that God's rest does not signify total passivity but rather a change in activity. On day 7 God *begins* a new activity.

GOD'S RULE: THE BEGINNING OF HIS ETERNAL ACTIVITY

On day 7, God begins to rule *over* creation. God's "rest" is a sign of God's "rule." The two cannot be separated. Consider this illustration. The shift of activity, or resting, is akin to a master chef who, having prepared an elaborate banquet, now sits down at the head of the table to partake of the feast. Ceasing from his labors as a chef does not imply a lapse into inactivity before the spread. Rather, the chef's rest signals a *new* activity — the active enjoyment of what he has prepared. And so it is with God's rest after the work of creation is finished. His rest is but the beginning of a new activity, his rule.

Perhaps your father was like my father.[4] My father had a chair. It was his own chair, a comfortable leather armchair placed in the living room near the fireplace, with the Bible and his newspaper nearby. His eight children were allowed to sit in it, but when we saw him coming, we scattered. Dad would ease into his chair, put his feet up on the ottoman, and rest. He might read, then close his eyes. It looked like he was resting from the busyness of the day. It was not, however, a passive rest. Although his eyes might be closed, my father knew what was going on, and he could be out of the chair in a moment! When

Dad was in his chair, however, life was good. It meant everything was under control—under *his* control; because from that chair my father governed. It was obvious to everyone in our home that he was the ruler of his family. He sustained our household, and life under his rule was very good indeed.

The idea that God, as the Father of all humanity, intends to rule over the entire creation, has staggering implications for big questions of meaning and purpose. For the resting rule of God speaks to the ultimate purpose or meaning for which everything had been made. The six creation days were heading somewhere after all—to life under the rule of God. History is moving toward the seventh-day rule of God. That is where we find meaning. Figuratively speaking, when God rests he steps to his throne. He eases his massive shoulders into the corners of the universe; he sprawls his feet across a galactic ottoman; *and he governs.* From that chair he not only sustains the whole created order, he gives it his divinely intended purpose.

Put simply, every king must have a kingdom. And for six days God created his kingdom, all the vast array. He ordered every relationship in a particular way, appointing *this* over *that*, and appointing man as "vassal king" over it all—and himself over man. And then, on day 7, he begins his powerful work of upholding and governing all those relationships. When God rests, he rules. And when we live under that rule we find purpose, meaning, and value. When God rules, life is good.

THE SURPRISING NATURE OF GOD'S RULE

Now, if we are to find ultimate meaning and purpose in learning to live under God's resting rule, it is only natural to ask, "What does that rule look like? Just how good is God's rule? From these verses in chapter 2 we think two surprising characteristics of God's rule can be clearly observed. First, God's rule provides us with ultimate meaning *unlike anything else* we might be tempted to substitute in its place. And second, God's rule over his creation is something that will *extend into eternity.*

Surprise #1: God's Rule Is Holy

God's seventh-day rule, and the meaning it provides us, is so good that he himself calls it *holy*. Genesis 2:3 says, "And God blessed the seventh day and called it holy." Perhaps you are familiar with the biblical word "holy."

"Holy" simply means "set apart." We can understand this meaning of the word in the context of verse 3: "And God blessed the seventh day and made it *holy*, because on it he rested from all the work of creating that he had done." Although there are seven days in a week, God chooses one of those days and sets it apart from the other six. He appropriates it to himself, like the mother or father who bakes special cookies and sets them on the highest shelf, out of the way of ordinary household traffic. Not only does he set it apart, he stamps it with his pleasure and sets it so high above men and women that they cannot touch it. God's rule — and the special day that points to it — are *holy*, set apart and above everything else.

The implication for those of us seeking meaning in life is clear. Since God has set apart the seventh day for his holy rule, therefore, everything and everyone will find meaning by setting themselves apart to live under that rule as he reveals it to us.

Not only is God's rule set apart from the rest of creation; it is also incorruptible. This is the second nuance of meaning to the word "holy." His rule is pure and uncontaminated by anything he has made. These two nuances of meaning are not unconnected in the context of Genesis 1. For when God separates day 7, the day of his rest, from days 1–6, he separates his rule *from* creation in order that his rule will never be corrupted *by* creation.

If the created order were ever to rebel against God himself, God's rule would remain secure and intact. For this reason it would be foolish to seek meaning in anything other than God. God's rule is unshakable — he can never be shaken off the throne anyway. God's rule is incorruptible; it offers us a meaning distinct from anything else in all of creation.

Surprise #2: God's Rule Is Eternal

The nature of God's rule extends beyond ideas of being set apart for God and settling for nothing other than God in answer to our search for meaning. For as we shall now see, the nature of God's rule, and the meaning we derive from living under it, extend to something we shall experience into all eternity. We are all heading toward the ultimate goal of God's seventh day of rest. The implications that we were created with this eternal purpose in mind are mind-boggling, and they will take a moment to unfold.

To get the feel for a never-ending rest, recall the anticipation of looking forward to an extended weekend. Is there any feeling quite like that on a Friday afternoon before a three-day weekend? The prospect of an extended vacation is even better. In Genesis 2 God enjoys a very long weekend indeed. His seventh day goes on forever!

The description of day 7 in the text is markedly different from the other six. If you look carefully at the account in Genesis 1, you will find a refrain that concludes each day of creation:

> "*And there was evening, and there was morning* — the first day." (v. 5)

> "*And there was evening, and there was morning* — the second day." (v. 8)

> "*And there was evening, and there was morning* — the third day." (v. 13)

*"And there was evening, and there was morning—*the fourth day." (v. 19)

*"And there was evening, and there was morning—*the fifth day." (v. 23)

*"And there was evening, and there was morning—*the sixth day." (v. 31)

Now look at day 7:

By the seventh day God had finished the work he had been doing; so on the seventh day he rested from all his work. And God blessed the seventh day and made it holy, because on it he rested from all the work of creating that he had done (2:2-3).

There is *no refrain.* Don't miss this discovery! The writer did not accidentally leave out the recurrent phrase, *"And there was evening, and there was morning . . ."* In this carefully crafted text there is no closure to day 7. After six workdays, God gave himself a day of everlasting rest: God's rest, and therefore God's rule, is *eternal.* It is ongoing.

In essence, God never stopped working! Certainly this is how Jesus understood God's day 7. Centuries after the writing of Genesis, he claimed that God is always working, even on the Sabbath. He grounded this claim in his understanding of Genesis 2:2-3.[5]

Some Implications for the Tradition of Biblical Literalism

What are the implications of 2:2-3 for biblical literalism? Remember, biblical literalism is a tradition that views the six days in Genesis 1 as twenty-four-hour time periods. Now, if it is true that day 7 has no end, the implications for the way in which biblical literalists read chapter 1 are significant. For example, one of the first questions that a modern reader asks when approaching this text is, "How long are the days?" Once we realize that the seventh day of Genesis 2:2-3 is no ordinary day, and that God's rest is not the same as our rest, but perhaps only analogous to it, we will begin to question the meaning of "day" in chapter 1.[6] These are not days as human beings commonly construe them. Rather, they are God's days, as he construes them.

The Copy and the Original

The difficulty biblical literalists have in viewing the length of days as anything other than twenty-four-hour periods, may arise from a very simple misunderstanding. Perhaps they tend to think that God's days are like our days; our days last twenty-four hours, therefore, so must God's. But perhaps the opposite is true: Perhaps our days are like God's days.[7] The question really is, which is a copy of which—which "rest" (human or divine) is the copy and which is the original?[8]

In his book Pilgrim's Regress, C. S. Lewis considers the whole issue of "which is the original and which is the copy," and suggests a clever solution to the conundrum. In Lewis's interesting logic, what is "foul" (or of lesser quality) is always a copy of what is "fair" (or of greater quality). According to this standard, our days must be based on God's days.[9] Our text offers further support to this reasoning. According to the writer, there are three full "days" of creation before the measurement of time as we construe it is even possible—the sun is not created until day 4! These cannot be days as human beings commonly construe them. Rather, these are God's days as he construes them. Our days are analogous to his days.

As Graeme Goldsworthy has pointed out, the key question of Genesis 1 "is not *whether* the Bible tells the truth, but *how* it tells it."[10] God created the earth in God's time, in his days. And those days are not necessarily limited to twenty-four-hour periods.

FINAL THOUGHTS

Day 7 is a surprising day. It presents many challenges to contemporary traditions. But how refreshing it is to hear from Genesis! The universe was created with divinely intended meaning. All creation was set apart to dwell everlastingly under God's rule.

What would block a man or woman from surrendering to God's eternal rest—his holy rule? Perhaps it would be the now-familiar barrier of our traditions. The teaching of Genesis is that *God rules from the center.* He will have it no other way. But do you see that our traditions tend to push God away from the center? They tend to displace him, replacing God's voice with other voices. Genesis 2:2-3 helps us to place God back at the center, and it requires that we push our traditions and self-made approaches to life to the periphery. It relocates God to his rightful place—upon the throne, over the heavens and the earth, and over every one of us. Meaning is to be found in living under that rule.

And so, with the restful rule of God over all creation, the prologue to Genesis comes to an end. The seven days are now completed. In the short span of one chapter plus three verses, we have encountered surprise after surprise.

⁴This is the account of the heavens and the earth when they were created.

When the LORD God made the earth and the heavens – ⁵and no shrub of the field had yet appeared on the earth and no plant of the field had yet sprung up, for the LORD God had not sent rain on the earth and there was no man to work the ground ⁶but streams came up from the earth and watered the whole surface of the ground – ⁷the LORD God formed the man from the dust of the ground and breathed into his nostrils the breath of life, and the man became a living being.

⁸Now the LORD God had planted a garden in the east, in Eden; and there he put the man he had formed. ⁹And the LORD God made all kinds of trees grow out of the ground – trees that were pleasing to the eye and good for food. In the middle of the garden were the tree of life and the tree of the knowledge of good and evil.

¹⁰A river watering the garden flowed from Eden; from there it was separated into four headwaters. ¹¹The name of the first is the Pishon; it winds through the entire land of Havilah, where there is gold. ¹²(The gold of that land is good; aromatic resin and onyx are also there.) ¹³The name of the second river is the Gihon; it winds through the entire land of Cush. ¹⁴The name of the third river is the Tigris; it runs along the east side of Asshur. And the fourth river is the Euphrates.

¹⁵The LORD God took the man and put him in the Garden of Eden to work it and take care of it. ¹⁶And the LORD God commanded the man, "You are free to eat from any tree in the garden; ¹⁷but you must not eat from the tree of the knowledge of good and evil, for when you eat of it you will surely die."

¹⁸The LORD God said, "It is not good for the man to be alone. I will make a helper suitable for him."

¹⁹Now the LORD God had formed out of the ground all the beasts of the field and all the birds of the air. He brought them to the man to see what he would name them; and whatever the man

called each living creature, that was its name. ²⁰*So the man gave names to all the livestock, the birds of the air and all the beasts of the field.*

But for Adam no suitable helper was found. ²¹*So the* LORD *God caused the man to fall into a deep sleep; and while he was sleeping, he took one of the man's ribs and closed up the place with flesh.* ²²*Then the* LORD *God made a woman from the rib he had taken out of the man, and he brought her to the man.*

²³*The man said,*

> *"This is now bone of my bones*
>> *and flesh of my flesh;*
> *she shall be called 'woman,'*
>> *for she was taken out of man."*

²⁴*For this reason a man will leave his father and mother and be united to his wife, and they will become one flesh.*

²⁵*The man and his wife were both naked, and they felt no shame.*

—GENESIS 2:4-25

5

MUD AS MAN

O ne of life's big questions is, "Who are we, really?" We have heard the prologue to Genesis (1:1–2:3) thunder forth an answer: "You, O *man* and *woman, you* are the pinnacle of God's creation. You alone are his crowning jewel!"

As we now turn the page to Genesis 2:4, we may wonder what will come next from the voice of Genesis. What we find are fresh spring rains that water and nurture the seeds of human dignity planted in chapter 1. The prologue (1:1–2:3) and the balance of chapter 2 (vv. 4-25) serve one overarching purpose and complement each other perfectly.[1] Perhaps giving you an illustration from my childhood will help clarify this.[2]

TWO MAPS, ONE JOURNEY

I vividly recall taking family vacations. My father was a schoolteacher, and summertime meant extended driving trips. We began at home in Chicago and drove to South Dakota and Mount Rushmore — across to Cheyenne — up to Yellowstone — down through the Rockies — and into Silverton, where we would camp for an extended time.

In the months leading up to those trips, Dad would always post a large map of the United States on our refrigerator door. This map contained the grand view of the entire journey. For on it, with indelible ink, Dad would trace our path. However, he never traced it out all at once. You see, all seven of us kids would set aside money from our newspaper routes in an effort to help pay for the gasoline for the trip. So, as the funds for gas accumulated, the indelible ink indicating how far we could go extended across the map. It was always a great day when the ink made its way back to the beginning, because we knew then that we had collected enough money to pay for the entire trip.

A funny thing, though: We never brought *this map* on the trip. The "grand view map" was too general. For the actual trip we needed a more detailed map, so we took along our *Rand McNally Road Atlas,* complete with all fifty states! I loved *that map* because it contained inset maps of large cities and all kinds of information the refrigerator map didn't have.

The creation account in Genesis 1, like the map on my family's refrigerator, is the grand view in which mankind is seen as the pinnacle, but only within the context of all of creation. Chapter 2, on the other hand, is like one page of the *Rand McNally* map, which shows in full detail what the pinnacle (mankind) is really like.

In one breath, chapter 1 spoke of the creation of man in the image of God as male and female. Now, however, beginning in 2:4, the writer focuses our attention specifically on humankind. He wants us to *camp here for an extended time.*

This is exciting, because chapter 2 deals directly with one of life's big questions: "Who are we, really?"

WE ARE DIVINE DUST

Genesis 2:7 says, "The LORD God formed the man from the dust of the ground." Notice the wording here: "*The LORD God formed the man from the dust . . .*" The plain sense of the text is clear and unmistakable: Men and women are creatures who have been made by God from the dust of the earth.[3] And while there is room for discussion regarding precisely *how* God did this (there were no video cameras at creation!), one thing is strenuously argued by the writer of Genesis: *Humanity traces its origin to the work of God.*

The notion of humanity as divine dust has been seriously challenged. With the publication of Charles Darwin's *The Origin of Species* and then his later book, *The Descent of Man*, the intellectual communities of Europe and America began in earnest to explain the origin of mankind from completely natural causes.

A splendid little paragraph from a not-so-well-known letter of Charles Darwin exudes his growing confidence in this theory. Darwin writes:

> It is often said that all the conditions for the first production of a living organism are now present, which could ever have been present. But if (and oh! what a big if!) we could conceive in some warm little pond, with all sorts of ammonia and phosphoric salts, light, heat, electricity, etc., present, that a proteine [*sic*] compound was chemically formed ready to undergo still more complex changes, at the present day such matter would be instantly devoured or absorbed, which would not have been the case before living creatures were formed.[4]

Darwin was convinced that his "what a big if" for the origin of life eventually would be documented. He was one of the first to credibly explain the creation of humanity *naturally*, without a creating God. According to Darwin's naturalism we are not divine dust, but merely dust.

However, one very perplexing question arises from the dust: How does naturalism explain the fact that people everywhere ask life's big questions? Why do we ask, *Why?* If we are merely dust, how are we capable of asking questions that touch on purpose? The writer Kurt Vonnegut, Jr., teases naturalism in this witty parody of Genesis 1:

> In the beginning God created the earth, and he looked upon it in its cosmic loneliness.
>
> And God said, "Let Us make creatures out of mud, so mud can see what We have done." And God created every living creature that now moveth, and one was man. Mud as man alone could speak. God leaned close as mud as man sat up, looked around and spoke. Man blinked. "What is the *purpose* of all this?" he asked politely.
>
> "Everything must have a purpose?" asked God.
>
> "Certainly," said man.
>
> "Then I leave it to you to think of one for all this," said God. And he went away.[5]

Vonnegut is showing the dilemma of humanity being created by an impersonal universe. How does *mere dust* come forth asking *What* and *Why?*

Isn't it at least possible that humanity was created by God with purpose? After all, matter is nothing more than matter, while people continually wrestle with purpose. At the end of the day, naturalism makes too little of mankind. This is the exalted teaching of Genesis: People, all people, are God's people. We are divine dust.

WE ARE UNDER DIVINE RULE

In Genesis 2:16 we read, "And the LORD God *commanded* the man . . ." The implications of this verse are striking. There is a *relationship* between humanity and God, with proper lines of *authority*. Although we are to rule over all the rest of creation, we ourselves are under divine rule.

The man and his Creator God are not equals. God asserts his authority over mankind very early in human history. Admittedly, the word "authority" leaves a bad taste in the mouths of many today. We don't like to be told what to do. We want to decide things for ourselves.

Nevertheless, Genesis asserts that God lays down rules with regard to what the first man and woman can and cannot do in the garden. According to Genesis, humanity is not autonomous. Although we rule over the created order, we too have a ruler.

Our Claim to Autonomy

Evidently, according to Genesis, we humans are not autonomous. The God who created us also rules over us through his Word. This teaching runs directly against the climate of our time. If you were to stop someone on the street and ask, "Excuse me, how would you answer the question, 'Who are you, really?'" surely few would respond with anything like, "I am divine dust and am to live under God's divine rule." No, today we want to live as if we were completely autonomous and free to create our own sets of rules.

For example, a recent television program spotlighted the controversial hiring of a professor at an East Coast school. This professor asserts that society ought to have the right to kill very young children (between birth and about six months) for various reasons. His rationale is rooted in his belief that up to that age children have not developed a moral capacity and therefore are not quite human beings. He is calling for us to live autonomously—to decide for ourselves what constitutes being human.

On another front, we are by now all too familiar with Dr. Kervorkian's rationale for assisted suicide: "It's their body! Why can't they do what they want with it?" If his premise is correct,

then his rationale stands; but if his premise is wrong—if we are
not our own, if we are to live under divine rule—then our present approach to euthanasia is in need of a massive overhaul.
Before deciding on a question such as euthanasia, we would
need to hear from God.

The teaching of Genesis is at odds with these modern views:
We are, at the most fundamental level, to live under the *commands* of the God who created us.

It is striking that the book of Genesis, written so many years
ago, bubbles with contemporary application. Consider whether
the poet Charles Swinburne was correct when he penned his
famous "hymn":

> Thou art smitten, thou God, thou art smitten,
> thy death is upon thee, O Lord.
> And the love-song of earth as thou diest,
> resounds through the wind of her wings—
> Glory to Man in the highest!
> For Man is the Master of things.[6]

Is man the master of things? Are we autonomous creatures
who live under our own word? The Bible says no.

Or, was Christopher Marlowe correct when he put forth this
syllogism?

> Man is the measure of all things.
> I am a man.
> Therefore, I am the measure of all things.[7]

Am "I" the measure of all things? Again, the Bible says no.
Humanity was created to live under God's divine rule. People
who desire to live autonomously often overlook the unfortunate
implications that come along with this lifestyle.

Implications of Autonomy

When we look at the traditions that have been handed down to us, we find a skewing of the Genesis teaching that mankind was uniquely created to live under the rule of God. Interestingly, naturalism *makes too little* of mankind while pervasive supernaturalism makes *too much* of mankind. Do you remember the premise of pervasive supernaturalism? It is that you yourself are divine, that you are autonomous—that as "God" you create all things and are over all things, and will one day be subsumed into that one substance called the Divine. Doesn't that seem to make too much of ourselves? The writer of Genesis insists that while we are made in the image of God, that is not to be confused with *being* God. God is autonomous; we are not. He alone is divine; we are divine dust.

And what of the tradition of naturalism? Clearly, autonomy is the chosen view within this tradition. Ironically, however, naturalism ends up thinking *too little* of men and women. The advocate of naturalism must in the end answer the question "Who are we, really?" with "We are really nothing more than dust!" We are accidental mutations that descended from a more primitive life-form millions of years ago.

The biblical teaching on who you are—your identity as a human being—is that you are *divine* dust. Yes, you are of the earth, and you will return to the earth. But you are also more than that. The Lord God formed you, uniquely, and intends to live in relationship to you. The Lord God put you here for his divine purposes. And you are meant to live under his divine rule. Genesis puts humanity in its true and proper place. It stays clear of thinking too much of ourselves as pervasive supernaturalism does or too little of ourselves as naturalism does.

So, to come back to our question, "Who are we, really?" Genesis responds with a refreshing summer rain that clears the air of the stifling humidity of our traditions. We are divine dust. We are uniquely made to live under divine rule, and as we shall see, we are created especially for a divinely orchestrated relationship.

WE ARE DIVINELY CREATED FOR RELATIONSHIP

Mankind's Relationship to the Created Order

In Genesis 2:18 the Lord God said, "It is not good for the man to be alone. I will make a helper suitable for him." Surprisingly, just after those words the reader of Genesis turns off the highway to travel some back roads.

Having read in verse 18 that God was going to make a helper suitable for the man, we would expect the next line to be something like, "So, God made the first woman." However, she doesn't come until verse 21. Instead, the writer asks us to follow him down the back roads of verses 19 and 20 to show us the man naming all the animals! As Bob Dylan sings,

> Man gave names to all the animals,
> In the beginning, long time ago.[8]

The question is, why this excursion? The answer is, in part, that it shows mankind's proper relationship to the created order: Men and women rule over all creation because humanity alone bears God's image. The recently released children's book *In Our Image: God's First Creatures* takes creative liberties with the text in setting forth its own view of Genesis 2. An ad for the book describes it this way:

> In this version [of the Genesis account], the animals of the earth welcome the news that God is going to create man and woman to share the world with them, and each contributes a characteristic gift to the newcomers — the tiger offers

courage, the lamb gentleness, the swan gracefulness, the chimpanzee curiosity, and so on. It's a simple story, charmingly told. . . .[9]

According to this book, the animals are conferring their characteristics upon the man; it recasts mankind in the image of the animals instead of the image of God. Although the story line is creative and perhaps even fun, its message distorts the voice of Genesis. It places the animal kingdom above humanity, which is precisely what this text of the Bible is *not* teaching.

Man's Relationship to Woman

God directed man to name the animals, not only to show the proper relationship between himself and the created order, but, more importantly, to show that the man was still without a suitable earthly relationship for himself. Genesis 2:20 confirms this:

But for Adam no suitable helper was found.

In essence, the back roads of the narrative show a prelude of preparation—the man needed to see that even though the animal kingdom was wide indeed, he was without a suitable partner. God wanted the man to know that he was made for a particular relationship.

Part of what it means to be made in the image of God is that we are made male and female. In the Bible, primeval mankind consists of two creatures meant to live in relationship to each other.[10]

This idea of relationship is very significant. A biblical understanding of the creation of man as male and female is critical to so many issues today. God gave the first man someone suitable for him, that is, a created being similar to himself. There were, however, differences between these two creatures.

God did not create another man for Adam. He created a woman. The text states this quite plainly. And in a world that swirls with dialogue on human sexuality, the voice of Genesis needs further consideration.

The climax of chapter 2 is found in verse 22: "Then the LORD God made a woman from the rib he had taken out of the man, and he *brought* her to the man." The language is nearly that of a wedding processional. Can you picture it? The man is waiting in the garden—the woman is clinging to the arm of God—the Lord God brings her to the man—the man, taking her hand in his for the first time, is out of his mind with happiness—and words pour forth from his lips in song:

> This is now bone of my bones
>   and flesh of my flesh;
> she shall be called "woman,"
>   for she was taken out of man.

Here we have the climactic moment of God's creative work—a picture of beauty, wonder, mystery, and magic. It is here, in the garden, that we find God's people dwelling in God's place under God's rule. And they are filled with gratitude! There is no sense of any problem, nor any hint that there ever will be a problem. The man and woman are naked. They feel no shame. They are without sin. They feel no guilt. They are in love. They are one flesh. What a beautiful ending to the detailed map of the creation narrative, the map which highlights humanity as the pinnacle of God's creation.

FINAL THOUGHTS

We began this chapter by looking into Genesis 2 for the answer to one of life's big questions: "Who are we, really?" After looking at the text, we hope you see that Genesis is full of fresh ideas.

And whether or not you agree with all of its teachings, you must admit that the answers it gives frame a storehouse of material for today's traditions to interact with. In response to the question, "Who are we, really?" Genesis 2 replies:

- We are divine dust.

- We are to live under divine rule.

- We are divinely created for relationship.

Thus far, the voice of Genesis.

¹*Now the serpent was more crafty than any of the wild animals the LORD God had made. He said to the woman, "Did God really say, 'You must not eat from any tree in the garden'?"*

²*The woman said to the serpent, "We may eat fruit from the trees in the garden, ³but God did say, 'You must not eat fruit from the tree that is in the middle of the garden, and you must not touch it, or you will die.'"*

⁴*"You will not surely die," the serpent said to the woman. ⁵"For God knows that when you eat of it your eyes will be opened, and you will be like God, knowing good and evil."*

—GENESIS 3:1-5

6

THE INTOXICATING
PROGRAM

W e finished the last chapter with the words "Thus far, the voice of Genesis." We have seen that the voice of Genesis is intimately connected to the voice of God. It was God's voice that sang creation into existence. It was God who fashioned mankind from the dust of the earth. It was God who ruled over all of creation through his Word. In essence, *God* has been the central character on the stage. He is the actor who commands the attention of every reader. And from stage center this actor proclaims the goodness of what his Word has created.

Life is good in the garden. The trees yield a plentiful supply of fruit. All the animals have names. The man is no longer alone. He rejoices in his wife—his soulmate and helper—as he boisterously sings the refrain, "Bone of my bone! Flesh of my flesh!" Everything in God's new world is good.

With the advent of chapter 3, however, something changes. The shift is signaled by the word "now" in verse 1. Suddenly and unnervingly, the protagonist of Genesis has left the stage. He is in the wings. His voice silent. The antagonist has taken the stage, and a new voice is heard in the garden. It is the voice of the serpent.

"Is God good?" the serpent inquires. "Should you really live under his Word?" Thus he propels the drama toward its fatal climax.

Genesis 3 deals with the first temptation humanity faces, namely the temptation to *doubt God's goodness* and to *reject God's Word.*

THE TEMPTATION TO DOUBT GOD'S GOODNESS

On the surface, the question the serpent asks seems innocent enough. It is a simple question, addressed to the woman: "Did God really say, 'You must not eat from any tree in the garden?'" In reality, the question is not innocent at all. In fact, it is hardly a question. The serpent is not seeking information. His sole intention, rather, is to instill doubt regarding God's goodness.

In Hebrew the true nature of the question is much clearer than in English. As Martin Luther emphasizes, "I cannot translate the Hebrew either in German or in Latin; the serpent uses the words 'aph-ki' as if to turn up its nose to jeer and scoff at one."[1] The intention behind the question is not to get an answer but to make a mockery of God's goodness.

The serpent implies that God is limiting the freedom of the man and the woman. "Would a *good* God restrict what you can and cannot eat?" "Would a *good* God withhold things from you?" "Would a *good* God limit your access to anything which he previously proclaimed *good?*"

The serpent's question is like a teenager asking a friend, "Did your parents *really* say you had to be home by ten o'clock?" The one asking the question is really making a statement: "You're sixteen years old. Your parents are putting excessive limits on your freedom. Think for yourself. *You* know what's good for you."

The meaning behind the serpent's question is now evident: Any divine limitations upon human freedom must be a bad thing.

In reality, the serpent plays fast and loose with the goodness of God by distorting the words of God. God had not forbidden the man and the woman to eat from *any* tree in the garden, as the serpent's question claims. Rather, God had put all kinds of trees in the garden expressly for them to enjoy. There was only *one* tree that was off-limits — the tree of the knowledge of good and evil. Do you see how the serpent distorts God's words? He is twisting the truth. His words are *not* what God actually had said.

Another voice has spoken. It is not the voice of God. It is not the voice of goodness and blessing, of power and rule. Rather, it is the voice of the antagonist. Like a spider, he has spun his web. His words have lured his victim near. The thread-like fibers of evil are spreading across the garden. The implications of the account in Genesis 3:1-5 are weighty. Let us consider two: the literary genre of Genesis, and the origin of evil.

Implications for Literary Genre

First, what kind of literature is this? What are we to make of a talking serpent? Is this allegory? Or mythology? Or is it an actual historical record? Is this a real snake, or does the writer cast the serpent as a metaphor, merely a symbol? [2]

Now, some might argue that you can't have it both ways — the serpent cannot be both a real snake and a metaphorical snake at the same time. It cannot be both a symbol and the thing symbolized. The account must be either historical or allegorical.

C. S. Lewis has spoken to this kind of dilemma. In another context he has written,

> When you accepted the exodus of Israel from Egypt as a type of the soul's escape from sin, you did not on that account abolish the exodus as a historical event. . . . It is a mischievous error to suppose that in an allegory the author is "really" talking about the thing symbolized, and not at all about the thing that symbolizes; the very essence of art is to talk about both.[3]

The tradition of biblical Christianity would argue, along the lines of Lewis's thinking, that the writer of Genesis 3:1-5 is speaking both of the symbol (the serpent) and of that which it symbolizes (which will be explained below). As literature, the Bible is capable of holding these literary complexities in tension.

Implications for the Origin of Evil

There is another implication that is even weightier. It has to do with the presence of evil in this garden paradise, which raises another set of questions for today's reader: How did another voice enter the garden? Where does evil come from? Why is there pain and suffering in God's very good world? If there is a God, why doesn't this God eliminate evil?

Such questions have confounded thinking people not only in our own time but throughout the centuries. All traditions have grappled with these questions. And at the end of the day, they fall short of providing answers that would satisfy us.

Simply put, Genesis 3:1-5 does not tell us how evil found its way onstage. The presence of evil in the garden is left a mystery. The voice of Genesis seems unconcerned with answering our questions, important though they may be. We are left, therefore, to our own conjecture.

We acknowledge that the above paragraph will not satisfy all the readers of this book. The silence of Genesis on the origin of evil is frustrating! The highly respected historian Paul Johnson gives voice to our frustration in his recent book *The Quest for God: A Personal Pilgrimage.* In his chapter on why evil exists, he asks,

> If God is infinitely good, and infinitely powerful too, why should evil exist at all, when it is within his capacity to eliminate it once and for all?[4]

Certainly this question is appropriate for those of us who

are asking life's big questions. It deserves a satisfactory response. While a definitive answer is beyond the scope of this book, we do find these words from G. K. Chesterton's *Orthodoxy* to be of help:

> According to most philosophers, God in making the world enslaved it. According to Christianity, in making it He set it free. God had written, not so much a poem, but rather a play ... which had necessarily been left to human actors and stage managers, who had since made a great mess of it.[5]

God set his creation free because God is love. If God is to be *loved* by mankind, he knows that love must be freely given. For love is a choice; it is volitional. Men and women must be capable of *not* loving God, if they are to love him freely. This is the point, also, behind Chesterton's play *The Surprise*,[6] in which God creates living creatures with a capacity to act freely rather than like robots, which have no capacity for love.

For many today, Chesterton's rationale for the possibility of evil is offensive. To state that evil exists because God is love seems incongruous with all that we know love to be. "If I were this loving God," says today's reader, "I would, because of love, eradicate the presence of evil from the world immediately."

Let's follow this thought for a moment: You are God. You are all-powerful. You are all-loving. You determine, on the count of three, to eliminate the presence of evil from the world. This would, of course, require not only eliminating evil from the present situation but also barring its effects on the future, forever. So tell us: What remains after you count to three? Certainly not people. Because all of humanity — every man and woman alive today — harbors the potential for evil.

Interestingly, of all our traditions, Christianity is the only worldview that offers a solution to the *persistence* of evil.

According to Christianity, this solution is first hinted at within this very chapter of Genesis, in verse 15. The solution finds *fulfillment* when Jesus of Nazareth conquers evil in his death and resurrection, and it will come to *culmination* when he returns to eliminate evil once and for all. Christianity, you see, proclaims that God postpones the elimination of evil from the world so that people like us might be rescued from judgment for our participation in that evil (see 2 Pet. 3:1-10).

Regardless of how our traditions attempt to address the problem of evil, the voice of Genesis does not allow us to place the blame on God. As we shall see more fully in the next chapter, the blame rests squarely on the shoulders of humanity. For it is the first man and woman — Adam and Eve — who will reject the Word of the Lord God.

The Temptation to Reject God's Word

While the voice of Genesis may not answer all our questions regarding the problem of evil, it does give us some insight into the personality of the serpent. He is crafty, cunning, duplicitous. He has greater designs on the man and the woman than merely tempting them to doubt God's goodness. Behind *his* words there is the unspoken desire for them to reject *God's* Word.

If the man and the woman were to give any real thought to the matter, they would understand the serpent's intention. For the serpent wants nothing less than the complete inversion of the creation order. The biblical pattern is that God had set up humanity to rule over the earth while God would rule over humanity by the power of his Word. To succumb to the serpent's temptation would be tantamount to stepping beyond the divine boundary God had set between the ruler and the ruled. They were created to be *God's* people, in *God's* place, living under *God's* Word. This is the arrangement that the serpent wants to undermine.

It is this Word of God that the serpent beckons Adam and Eve to disobey. He argues that they don't need to live under God's Word. They can be a law unto themselves—their own moral compass. They can be freed from the restrictions of an unkind God. In sum, they can become their own God.

It is easy to imagine that this temptation would seem right to Adam and Eve. After all, as the serpent reminds them, in eating the fruit they would "be like God." And were they not created in the image of God? Weren't they entitled to everything good? Would God want to withhold wisdom, which is a good thing, from them?

How quickly the voice of God fades in the minds of the man and the woman. It seems like years, perhaps, since he exited the stage. They have no recollection of his voice, no memory of the consequences he had laid out for the rejection of his Word. In its place there is a sudden and fierce desire to succumb to temptation.

Dietrich Bonhoeffer illustrates through his own experience the principle at work in the garden. He writes,

> With irresistible power desire seizes mastery over the flesh. All at once a secret, smoldering fire is kindled. The flesh burns and is in flames. It makes no difference whether it is sexual desire, or ambition, or vanity, or desire for revenge, or love of fame and power, or greed for money, or, finally, that strange desire for the beauty of the world, of nature. Joy in God is in course of being extinguished in us and we seek all our joy in the creature. At this moment, God is quite unreal to us, he loses all reality, and only desire for the creature is real; the only reality is the devil. Satan does not here fill us with hatred of God, but with forgetfulness of God. . . . It is here that everything within me rises up against the word of God.[7]

The man and the woman are filled with temptation's desire and have grown deaf to the Lord God's warning—that death, not life would accompany the rejection of his Word. His command was for their own welfare. He was looking out for their good, as a shield against the knowledge of evil.

The serpent's temptation is a cunning move and a monstrous lie. It is cunning because, as Derek Kidner has observed, "To be as God and to achieve it by outwitting God is an intoxicating program."[8]

And so, having accomplished his purpose, the voice of the serpent falls silent. The man and the woman stand alone in the spotlight, center stage. The next scene belongs to them. And in it they will follow either the Word of God or the voice of the serpent.

⁶*When the woman saw that the fruit of the tree was good for food and pleasing to the eye, and also desirable for gaining wisdom, she took some and ate it. She also gave some to her husband, who was with her, and he ate it.* ⁷*Then the eyes of both of them were opened, and they realized they were naked; so they sewed fig leaves together and made coverings for themselves.*

⁸*Then the man and his wife heard the sound of the LORD God as he was walking in the garden in the cool of the day, and they hid from the LORD God among the trees of the garden.* ⁹*But the LORD God called to the man, "Where are you?"*

¹⁰*He answered, "I heard you in the garden, and I was afraid because I was naked; so I hid."*

¹¹*And he said, "Who told you that you were naked? Have you eaten from the tree that I commanded you not to eat from?"*

¹²*The man said, "The woman you put here with me — she gave me some fruit from the tree, and I ate it."*

¹³*Then the LORD God said to the woman, "What is this you have done?"*

The woman said, "The serpent deceived me, and I ate."

—GENESIS 3:6-13

A SENSE OF ESTRANGEMENT

Nineteenth-century German philosopher Friedrich Nietzsche said, "All evidence of truth comes only from the senses."[1] Apparently, for a few crucial minutes, the man and the woman lived by Nietzsche's dictum. The senses—first sight and smell, then touch and taste—aroused in them an unstoppable rush. The fruit was there, pleasing to the eye and tempting to the palate. It looked so good! It held the promise of making them wise, like God. And so, in a quick, impulsive move, the man and the woman rejected God's Word and followed the voice of the serpent.

The writer of Genesis 3 describes the scene's action in rapid-fire language:

- She took it.

- She ate it.

- She gave it to her husband.

- He ate it.

For us, however, the scene unfolds as if suspended in time. The woman sees the fruit. It is full and ripe. Hesitantly, she

reaches for it. The skin is taut and unblemished, the aroma intoxicating. She grasps the fruit, and in one deft stroke pulls it from
the tree. The first bite is like ambrosia between her teeth—food
fit for the gods. "Here, Adam. You try it! It's good!" He follows
her lead, like a dumb lamb led to the slaughter.

The action is completed in a matter of seconds, but with consequences for the rest of time. Adam and Eve now gaze into the
abyss. They have eaten the forbidden fruit. And, in that fatal
meal, they have acted on a callous dissatisfaction with being
merely human. Wanting something better, they rebel against the
kingly Word of God and follow instead the voice of the serpent.
They are now fallen humanity, humanity as we know it today—
all too human. Genesis has spoken to answer another of life's big
questions: "What's the matter with people?"

The first man and woman have committed the first sin, and
the inescapable consequences of that sin impact everyone who
follows them.

CONSEQUENCES OF THE FIRST SIN

The Dislocation of Human Relationship

Nothing would ever be the same again. The man and the
woman, for the first time, experience dislocation in their relationship to each other. This can be seen in the preoccupation they
now have with their own bodies. Why this urge to cover up?
Why this shame and embarrassment in the presence of each
other? Before eating the forbidden fruit they had felt no need for
clothing. Now, according to Genesis 3:7,

> the eyes of both of them were opened, and they realized they
> were naked; so they sewed fig leaves together and made cov-
> erings for themselves.

Their shame is a signal that their relationship to each other has changed. Now they are painfully self-conscious. As an infant in his mother's womb needs no clothes, so Adam and Eve, wrapped in the warmth of God's presence, had no need for a covering. Now — as if thrust from the womb without warning — the impulse is to cover themselves and hide. What a contrast to how they felt earlier: "The man and his wife were both naked, and they felt no shame" (2:25).

The relational dislocation is seen not only in the *shame* they now feel, but also in the *blame* the man places on the woman. In Genesis 3:12 the man says, "the woman you put here with me — *she* gave me some fruit from the tree, and I ate it."

What a cowardly act!

The Dislocation of Divine Relationship

Adam and Eve's sinful condition is exposed — laid bare — before the presence of the Lord God. The dislocation of their relationship to God is evident as they try to hide from him — as they try to take cover in the late-afternoon shadows. They feel an overwhelming dread. *What have they done?* The fruit turns sour in their stomachs as the footsteps of God get closer and closer. His presence in the garden is so palpable that the trees rustle, even shiver as he passes. The phrase of verse 8, which is translated as "the sound of the LORD God," also can be rendered "the rustle of God." It is as if God, having entered the garden with the fullness of his majesty, leaves a wake of shimmering trees behind him.

The man and the woman retreat farther into the shadows, but in vain. The impulse to hide from God is an indication that their relationship with the divine has been fundamentally altered.

If their attempt to hide points to a dislocation from the divine, God's verbal confrontation confirms it. God knows what they have done, but he wants to hear it from their own lips. His questions are simple and pointed, almost clipped. They demand straightforward answers:

- Where are you?

- Who told you that you were naked?

- Have you eaten from the tree that I commanded you not to eat from?

- What is this you have done?

Every one of these questions points to Adam and Eve's guilt. Adam, however, resists the divine probe. His dislocated impulse is to cover his guilt. His answers, in fact, are anything but straightforward.

Can you imagine this scene? It would have been so simple to answer God's "Where are you?" with "Here I am, Lord." Straightforward. Honest. Humble. Manly. Instead, Adam answers evasively: "I heard you in the garden, and I was afraid because I was naked; so I hid" (v. 10). How much better it would have been to come clean: "Lord, I am hiding because I have sinned! I have eaten the fruit."

It is this confession that God wants to hear. And so, God makes the next move to draw it out: "Who told you that you were naked? Have you eaten from the tree that I commanded you not to eat from?" (v. 11).

God is bending over backwards to allow Adam to confess. He does not condemn the man without a hearing. He gives Adam room to acknowledge what he has done. God is making himself fully available to hear Adam's confession. But Adam will have none of it. The dislocation from the divine relationship is now as good as sealed.

Not satisfied with the man's admission, God now turns to the woman:

God: "What is this you have done?"

Eve: "The serpent deceived me, and I ate" (v. 13).

Like the man, the woman places blame elsewhere. Her own evasiveness is a sign of her dislocation from God.

There can be no mistaking the teaching of Genesis 3:6-13. To the question "What's the matter with people?" Genesis answers that all human relationships are now fractured. And what is worse, humanity's position is now one of alienation and estrangement — of man from woman, and of both from God.

Some Comments on the First Sin

The Man Is Held Responsible

It is striking to observe that God held Adam responsible for the first sin. One might expect God to place a greater portion of blame on Eve. After all, wasn't she the one who was tempted? Wasn't she the first one to eat? And didn't she offer the fruit to her husband? However, verse 9 clearly states that God confronted the *man* first: "But the LORD God called to the man, 'Where are you?'"

Adam is the one to whom God gave the command not to eat of the one tree; and he is the one God now holds responsible for the first sin. We know that he was by the woman's side as she ate the fruit. Verse 6 says, "She also gave some to her husband, who was with her, and he ate it." Moreover, the text implies that the man was present also at the temptation. In fact, the notion that Adam was with Eve during her conversation with the serpent is clear from verses 1, 4, and 5, where the serpent uses the *plural* form of the pronoun *you*.[2]

The Creation Order Is Inverted

It is interesting to see how God's perfect order, set forth in Genesis 1 and 2, is now in complete disarray. At creation, God ruled over humanity by *his* Word. And humanity was to exercise dominion over the rest of creation, including the animal world. Now, with the first sin, God's Word has been publicly discredited and undermined before all creation, and mankind, rather than ruling over the animal world, is subject to its leading.

"You Will Surely Die" Becomes Reality

In eating the forbidden fruit, Adam and Eve pulled the linchpin on their own gallows. For the serpent told a monstrous lie when he said to the woman, "You will not surely die." The first sin most assuredly brought death. A few pages later, in Genesis 5:5, we read, "Altogether, Adam lived 930 years, and *then he died.*"

But death, according to Genesis, is more than that which we experience physically. It is more than a physical separation from this life; it is primarily a *spiritual* separation from God. This spiritual separation will be portrayed dramatically when God banishes the man and the woman from his presence. The banishment from the garden points to a spiritual separation, for Adam and Eve are driven out of God's garden, away from his presence here on earth. The voice of Genesis will go on to show the full-blown effects of spiritual separation in the judgment of mankind in the flood. And, according to the Christian tradition, the flood prefigures the final judgment when God will eternally separate from himself everyone who, like Adam, rejects his Word.

American theologian Jonathan Edwards (1703–1758) spoke

to this idea of eternal separation from God as a logical outcome of mankind's sin:

> If Adam, for his persevering *obedience,* was to have had *everlasting life and happiness, in perfect holiness, union* with his Maker, and *enjoyment of his favour,* and this was the life which was to be confirmed by the tree of life; then, doubtless, the death threatened in a case of disobedience, which stands in direct opposition to this, was an exposure to *everlasting wickedness and misery, in separation* from God and in *enduring his wrath.*[3]

Of course, today's traditions reject such a dismal view of humanity's relationship to God. Today's voices claim that Christianity misreads the human condition.

Implications for the Nature of Man: Is Humanity Sinful?

Martin Gardner has written a provocative novel called *The Flight of Peter Fromm.* His plot line describes the progress of a university student (Peter Fromm) who, upon encountering the challenges of a secular education, begins to distance himself from the biblical tradition in which he was reared. Of particular concern is the view of Fromm's mentor-professor on that "Edwardsian" notion of human nature. At one point Fromm writes his professor,

> Dear Homer,
> I think the greatest lesson I've learned is that most men are good. Oh, I know there's plenty of cruelty and self-seeking in all of us, and if someone wants to call that original sin I suppose there's no harm in it. I'm convinced, though, that goodness is the stronger impulse. I think most people love more than they hate. . . . Maybe you're right about sin being no more than a mental illness that results from bad conditioning. I know this is what you've always tried to tell me. . . . I have no sense of estrangement. I can't believe that my loss of faith in orthodox Christianity is against God's will.[4]

Fromm puts forth his own answer to the question, "Is humanity sinful?" His answer is a simple no: sin is nothing more than a "mental illness that results from bad conditioning."

In contrast, orthodox Christian theologians have taught that all humanity—every man, woman, and child who has ever lived—has Adam's original sin within him or her. That is, we all have inherited the consequences of Adam and Eve's first sinful act of disobedience.

Is this idea unreasonable? Consider this illustration. Someday, when we are dead and buried, our children will receive an inheritance. Part of the inheritance will probably take the form of material goods. The weightier part, however, will consist of all the things, good and bad, that they have learned from our influence over their lives. Now, when Adam died, he left his children an inheritance, and that inheritance no doubt contained many good things. But he also passed on to them the sum of the effects of his own sinful disobedience, including a helpless and fatal tendency to fall into sin themselves. They, in turn, passed on this same inheritance to their children, who passed it on to their children, who—with the passage of time and generations—passed it on to you and me. This is what the Bible teaches.

We realize that such a teaching is not easy for a thinking person to swallow. It seems to be at odds with our modern, psychologically informed notions of humankind. Moreover, the biblical teaching strikes us as unfair. As the great mathematician Blaise Pascal once wrote, "There can be no doubt that nothing shocks our reason more than to say that the sin of the first man made guilty those who, so far from that source, seem incapable of having taken part in it. This contamination seems not only impossible to us, but also quite unjust.[5]" Nevertheless, this is the teaching of the tradition of Christianity.

FINAL THOUGHTS

And so in this chapter we have found ourselves once again face to face with one of life's big questions: "What is the matter with us?" We have heard from Genesis. We have heard from our modern representative, Peter Fromm. And now the question goes back to you, the reader. You must make your own decision as to your view of the nature of men and women.

Put differently, which view makes better sense of the world in which we live—the voice of Genesis, or the voice of Peter Fromm? Is humanity basically good? Or has moral corruption touched us all? Many years ago a famous correspondence in the *London Times* wrestled with these very issues. The editors of the newspaper asked individuals to respond to the question, "What is wrong with the world today?" The best letter of all was also the shortest. It read,

> Dear Sir,
> I am,
> Yours faithfully,
> G. K. Chesterton

Reader, do you believe that? If asked, "What is wrong with the world," would your response be, "I am?" You see, before you make a judgment on the rest of humanity, you must come to terms with the nature of yourself: Who are *you*, really?

To answer this question with honesty and integrity will be difficult. And it will require, as we shall see in the next chapter, leaving behind some of the most powerful and attractive voices of our time.

¹⁴So the LORD God said to the serpent, "Because you have done this,

> "Cursed are you above all the livestock
>   and all the wild animals!
> You will crawl on your belly
>   and you will eat dust
>   all the days of your life.
> ¹⁵And I will put enmity
>   between you and the woman,
>   and between your offspring and hers;
> he will crush your head,
>   and you will strike his heel."

¹⁶To the woman he said,

> "I will greatly increase your pains in childbearing;
>   with pain you will give birth to children.
> Your desire will be for your husband,
>   and he will rule over you."

¹⁷To Adam he said, "Because you listened to your wife and ate from the tree about which I commanded you, 'You must not eat of it,'

> "Cursed is the ground because of you;
>   through painful toil you will eat of it
>   all the days of your life.
> ¹⁸It will produce thorns and thistles for you,
>   and you will eat the plants of the field.
> ¹⁹By the sweat of your brow
>   you will eat your food
> until you return to the ground,
>   since from it you were taken;
> for dust you are
>   and to dust you will return."

²⁰Adam named his wife Eve, because she would become the mother of all the living.

²¹The LORD God made garments of skin for Adam and his wife and clothed them. ²²And the LORD God said, "The man has now become like one of us, knowing good and evil. He must not be allowed to reach out his hand and take also from the tree of life and eat, and live forever." ²³So the LORD God banished him from the Garden of Eden to work the ground from which he had been taken. ²⁴After he drove the man out, he placed on the east side of the Garden of Eden cherubim and a flaming sword flashing back and forth to guard the way to the tree of life.

—GENESIS 3:14-24

8

UTOPIAN DREAMS

At the conclusion of the last chapter we said that to embrace Christianity would require leaving behind some of the most powerful and attractive traditions of our time. This is difficult, because the way we think about God, the world, and our place in the world stems largely from those traditions passed down to us from preceding generations. We think the way we do about these important issues because the proponents of our traditions have taught us how to think.

THE POWER OF OUR TRADITIONS

In his delightful little book *Jesus Rediscovered*, Malcolm Muggeridge gives us a personal glimpse into the power preceding generations exert over us. He writes:

> I was brought up an ardent believer in the religion of this age—utopianism. My father used to read aloud to us on Sunday evenings from books like William Morris's *Earthly Paradise*. . . . I remember the scene vividly . . . my mother asleep in her chair, my father's voice rising and falling vigorously. . . . My clearest memory of him is at open air meetings, with his words rising above the noise of traffic as he held forth about the splendid world that lay ahead. . . . To me it all seemed absolutely clear and incontrovertible. . . . [S]chools of the kind that I attended would, I was confident, provide the enlightened citizenry for our New Jerusalem when it came to pass.[1]

Muggeridge leaves no doubt that his early beliefs about God, the world, and his place in the world came from the influence of his father. Young Malcolm's utopian fervor, his belief that we could fix all our problems, his adolescent expectation of an earthly paradise, his hope in the splendid world that lay ahead, his confidence of a New Jerusalem were all rooted in the intellectual voice of his father—a voice which rejected the Genesis story.

Today, as in Muggeridge's day, there is nearly a universal rejection of the Genesis story. We have outgrown the Genesis story. We rebel against Genesis 1 with its God who is Lord over all creation. We render Genesis 2 as farcical, with its man and woman made especially and intentionally by the hand of God. And if the seemingly outlandish claims of those chapters have not undermined our belief in such a God, Genesis 3 surely does so, with its ideas of a utopian garden spoiled by Adam and Eve's fall, of an earthly paradise now forever lost, and of a world and a citizenry far from enlightened, but rather, sullied with the stains of original sin.

And so, by the third chapter of Genesis the traditions of our time have abandoned all belief in this account. At this point in the narrative people raise their voices above the noise of disputation and proclaim: "No more talk on the first sin! No more preaching on human helplessness. No more fairy tales regarding serpents talking to women and God cursing snakes. No more notion of divine value and meaning. We don't believe it anymore! Instead we choose to believe that we are sound at heart—we can fix our own problems—we can yet achieve the greatest good for the greatest number of people. Moreover, we believe that if ultimate meaning is to be found in this world, it will come from our own triumphs over evil, not from God's intervention and rescue."

This is the bravado into which Muggeridge was born, and this is the tradition to which he later subscribed—a boundless confidence in human achievement that persists even to this day.

A Problem with Rejecting Genesis

There is, however, a problem with this view, despite its wide following. The utopian tradition *fails to square with the world as we know it.*

Some crucial questions with regard to our traditions come to mind. For example, is the heart of humanity, as you see it played out on your television screen each night, *good?* Are we really seeking the greatest good, or do our pursuits, both individually and corporately, advance our own personal and national interests?

And if God does not exist, as many of our traditions hold, can they please explain to us how it is that "mud as man" sits up and asks, "Why?" Would man—as merely matter—ask anything at all? Where does our moral compass come from?

"Come forward, utopian voices!" we might well demand, "How does your view account for the way the world is?"

The Power of Genesis

We ask you, the reader, to come forward too, for you are a thinking man or woman. Ask these questions of your traditions. Are you satisfied with their responses? Or are you surprised to discover that the opening chapters of Genesis offer thinking people a most plausible explanation regarding who we really are, what we have really done, where we are going, and how God responds to our human rebellion?

These chapters in Genesis have been teaching us that we are divine in some sense; indeed, we have been made in the image of God. Yet we are also dust, made from the stuff of this earth. Furthermore, we are told in Genesis that our first parents had a very special relationship with God—that they were to live under his Word—but that they rejected that special relationship.

Further, Genesis has told us that since we are *from* them, we are *like* them, in that each one of us continues to reject God's Word. We live as if it were not true, and as if it were not binding on us. The teaching of these chapters is that we have alienated ourselves from God.

We curse God. And interestingly, according to our text for this chapter, God curses back! Now *that* would account for the world as we know it to be. And that would account for our inability to fix all our problems.

A God Who Curses and Judges

Only a Cursing God Makes Sense of the World

It is an extraordinary thing — that God would curse his creation. Take a look at the text for yourself. Verse 14 says,

> So the LORD God said to the serpent, "Because you have done this, *cursed* are you!"

And in verse 17 he says to the man,

> "*Cursed* is the ground because of you."

What are we to make of a cursing God? Today, if and when the existence of God is acknowledged at all, God is said to be *all-loving*. However, does the idea of an all-loving God fit the picture of the world we see today? In fact, does not a *cursing* God make better sense of the world as we know it? For without such curses we most certainly would have built our New Jerusalem by now. Something — or someone — is thwarting our efforts. Doesn't it seem that way to you?

And a cursing God is precisely what Genesis proclaims. The writer of Genesis teaches us that *God* is thwarting our efforts — the God who made the heavens, the earth, and life itself, and pronounced it all good. And so, it is reasonable to ask, "Why would such a God curse his own creative work?"

According to the text, our sin is of such a degree that God withholds his blessing, indeed, that he sends forth his curses. God is angry toward our universal rejection of his rule. God curses our world because he will not permit us to fix all our problems; he will not allow us to live out the lie of autonomy — that is, to live our lives as if our Creator did not exist. This is what Genesis teaches.

The application of Genesis 3:14-24 can be put succinctly: *The world is as it is because we all are living under the judgments and curses of God.* God is at odds with humanity. Relationships between men and women are fractured as we continually find ourselves at odds with one another. Work is a never-ending struggle. And each one of us feels alone in the world.

Genesis 3:14-24 compels us to consider the first sin from God's perspective. For it is here that we confront the broad scope of God's judgment upon us for the willful rebellion against his rule.

God's Judgments on the Woman

As Eve tasted the forbidden fruit, her soul must have sensed the chilling change that now lay ahead. For the frigid winds of winter engulfed her for the first time. She was afraid — God was coming in judgment, as verse 16 of our text makes apparent:

> To the woman he said, "I will greatly increase your pains in childbearing; with pain you will give birth to children. Your desire will be for your husband, and he will rule over you."

Pain and subjection to her husband's rule are God's judgment upon the woman for her rebellion against his Word. John Milton said that discord is the daughter of sin.[2] The woman's life is now replete with discord, even amid experiences that should bring her the greatest pleasure, such as giving birth to her children.

Childbearing is not the only life experience marked by discord. As we have already seen in the last chapter, the relationship between the woman and the man is altered for the worse: The man will now *rule* over the woman.

This is a harsh judgment. That little phrase at the end of Genesis 3:16 — "and he will rule over you" — exacts a heavy price. The judgment for Eve's defiance of the divine will is this: She will have discord on every front, in bringing forth children and in her own marriage; for the man will now dominate the woman. The compatibility marked out by the creation order is now contorted into servility. Man will command woman for his own gratification.[3]

Isn't this the sad but realistic picture of the world in which we live? The scene is despicable; it is not the way we would have things to be. Yet, it is hard to contest that the Genesis account portrays a realistic picture of the world as we know it to be.

How Do Our Traditions Account for This Judgment?

How do the traditions that reject the Genesis story account for this perversion of male domination that weaves its way throughout human history? One would expect that the twentieth-century intellectuals who championed the wholesale rejection of God (and, in particular, this book of Genesis) would bring forth a better answer to this perverse reality. One would certainly expect that they themselves would show us a better way. Sadly, this is not the case.

Take Bertrand Russell, for example. Certainly no one would question Russell's rejection of the book of Genesis (and of religious faith in general). His disdain was so great that he perfected a parlor performance of something he called "The Atheist's

Creed." Paul Johnson in his book *Intellectuals* tells us that Russell
would recite, in the nasal tones of a chanting clergyman:

> We do not believe in *God*.
> But we believe in the supremacy
>   of *humanity*.
> We do not believe in life after *death*.
> But we believe in *immortality* —
> *Through good deeds*.[4]

For all the positive things that might be said about Russell, at
the end of the day, how did he treat women? Johnson goes on to
tell us:

> In theory Russell kept up with the twentieth-century move-
> ment to emancipate women; in practice he remained rooted in
> [the] nineteenth century.... Dora [one of his four wives] wrote
> of him, "Bertie did not really believe in the equality of women
> with men . . . he believed the male intellect to be superior to
> that of the female. He once told me that he usually found it
> necessary to talk down to women."[5]

Jean Paul Sartre was no better. Of his relationship with
Simone de Beauvoir we read,

> She served him as mistress, surrogate wife, cook and manager,
> female bodyguard and nurse. . . . [H]e was notoriously
> unfaithful. In the annals of literature, there are few worse
> cases of a man exploiting a woman.[6]

Do you see the sad point we are making? Those who espouse
a tradition other than Genesis with regard to why the world is
the way it is *are themselves — by the example of their own lives — argu-
ments for the veracity of the Genesis account.*

According to Genesis 3, a woman's life is marked,

appallingly, by discord and pain—*pain caused by sin*. This is the sad reality of the world in which we live. A woman's life is often a veil of tears. To paraphrase the words of Charles Swindoll, "If tears were indelible ink instead of clear fluid, [every woman in the world] would be stained for life."[7]

Genesis, while at times hard to take, nonetheless gives us a plausible answer regarding a woman's discord at home and difficulty in relationships. It is the judgment of God upon her willful sin.

God's Judgments on the Man

God's judgment for sin doesn't stop with the woman, however. She is not left alone in her pain. The man has his share as well. Read Genesis 3:17-19a (emphasis added):

> To Adam he said, "Because you listened to your wife and ate from the tree about which I commanded you, 'You must not eat of it,' *cursed* is the ground because of you; through painful toil you will eat of it all the days of your life. It will produce thorns and thistles for you, and you will eat the plants of the field. By the sweat of your brow you will eat your food."

The man will have difficulty in work. Interestingly, the word translated "pain" for the woman in verse 16 is repeated in verse 17 to refer to the man's "painful toil." Her pain in the home is likened to his pain in the workplace. Since his sin lay in eating the forbidden fruit of the garden, the land itself, which was created to sustain him, now rises up against him. The man's workplace is *cursed*. It is a fitting punishment, and from it the man will learn that he is not autonomous.

Studs Terkel opens his widely acclaimed book *Working* with these startling words:

This book, being about work, is by its very nature, about violence — to the spirit as well as to the body. It is about ulcers as well as accidents. About shouting matches as well as fist fights. About nervous breakdowns as well as kicking the dog around. It is, above all (or beneath all) about daily humiliations.[8]

What person who reads this is not familiar with the difficulties of the work environment? Look at the striking phrase in verse 19: "by the sweat of your brow." Man's attempt to live outside the rule of God results not in his becoming *like* God, as the serpent promised; rather, it results in a never-ending struggle for survival. Without God, there is little more than futility in our work. The twentieth-century mystic Simone Weil put it this way:

He exhausts himself in order that he may eat, and he eats in order that he may have the strength to work, and after a year of toil, everything is as it was when he began.[9]

Thus, we see the curse of God in the work of man.

How Do Our Traditions Account for This Judgment?

Now, what about our traditions that reject the Genesis account? Do the traditions that espouse another reason for why the world is as it is escape the state of affairs that this verse describes? No, they do not. Consider socialist writer Leonard Woolf's assessment of his personal work history:

I see clearly that I have achieved practically nothing. The world today and the history of the human anthill during the past 57 years would be exactly the same as it is if I had played ping pong instead of sitting on committees and writing books and memoranda. I have therefore to make a rather ignominious confession that I must have in a long life ground through between 150,000 and 200,000 hours of perfectly useless work.[10]

This is God's curse on man. Do you see what Genesis is teaching? *Our sin against God keeps us from realizing our dream of an earthly paradise.* There will be no paradise until there is no sin. God will not lift his curse until we live under his Word. And until we live under his Word, we are relegated to continual, monotonous discord and difficulty.[11]

THE FINAL JUDGMENT OF GOD

Physical Death

Not only discord, not only difficulty, not only dilemmas, but — for both the man and the woman — God pronounces a final judgment: *death.* Only in death will the woman and man's painful labor cease. Look at God's pronouncement of a death sentence (v. 19):

> "By the sweat of your brow you will eat your food until you return to the ground, since from it you were taken; for dust you are and to dust you will return."

You will surely die. Today you sit in a chair with blood coursing through your arteries and veins. The matter of your brain is hard at work. You see and hear, you move and speak, you have plans and loving relationships. Today you are alive! However, the day is coming when others will stand over your coffin. On that day the earth will be filled with people yet unborn — but *you* will have passed on into the everlasting night.

Death is God's judgment for sin, and nothing you possess can ever change that. Your rank and position in life will matter not. Your amassed wealth will amount to nothing. Death comes to us all. The last words of Elizabeth I, Queen of England, were:

> O my God! It is over. I have come to the end of it — the end, the end. To have only one life, and to have done with it. To have

lived and loved and triumphed; and now to know it is over!
One may defy everything but this![12]

Many today want to deny the reality of death. In fact, the
thought of dying compels some to run fast toward traditions that
deny God's existence. They are like Dr. Rieux, the character in
Camus' book *The Plague,* who spends his life fighting against the
world as he knows it to be. He says,

> Since the order of the world is shaped by death, mightn't it be
> better for God if we refuse to believe in Him and struggle with
> all our might against death, without raising our eyes toward
> heaven where he sits in silence?[13]

Today, people would rather grasp the nettles of this painful
world and allow the thorns and thistles to penetrate their hands
than to look up to where they might see God.

Spiritual Death

According to Genesis, death for people who refuse to look up
will be horrifying indeed. For the death of Genesis is spiritual as
well as physical. Know this: if there is a God, and if that God is
angry with you in your living, he will remain angry with you in
your dying. It has been said that Rabbi Johanan ben Zakkai, at
the time of his death,

> . . . lifted up his voice and wept: — "Were I going only to greet
> the face of a king of flesh and blood, his anger would . . . be for
> this world only; his chains — if he should cast me in prison —
> only for this world. If he killed me I should die to this world
> only, and perchance I could soothe him with words or bribe
> him with gold. But now I go to greet the face of the King of
> Kings, the Holy One — and if he be angry his wrath embraces
> both this world and the world to come; and him I may in no
> wise move with words nor bribe with gold.[14]

Imagine the horror of being banished from the presence of God into a land of everlasting curses—a place where everything you do, and everyone you know, works against your welfare, indefinitely and without respite. That is hell!

It is not an overstatement to say that hell is prefigured in Genesis 3. Discord, difficulty in life, and the inevitability of death are harsh punishments to bear. However, an even worse sentence is reserved for the man and the woman—the words of *banishment:*

> So the LORD God banished him from the Garden of Eden to work the ground from which he had been taken. After he drove the man out, he placed on the east side of the Garden of Eden cherubim and a flaming sword flashing back and forth to guard the way to the tree of life (Gen. 3:23-24).

FINAL THOUGHTS

Thus, Adam and Eve are banished from the garden. Paradise is lost. Milton describes the anguish of their departure:

> "O unexpected stroke, worse than death!
> Must I thus leave Thee, Paradise?
> thus leave Thee, native soil?
> these happy walks and shades. . . .
> How shall I part,
> and whither wander down
> into a lower world. . . .
> How shall we breathe in other air
> less pure . . . ?"[15]

The pathos of Milton mirrors the emotion of verse 24. Adam and Eve do not simply leave the garden. The wording is clear: They are forced out. Out! Out into the darkness. Sin will not be tolerated in the presence of God. And with the angels standing guard, the man and the woman are put on notice: *God is hostile toward outsiders.*[16] No intruders are permitted in the presence of God. He is hostile to all outsiders, and outsiders Adam and Eve now are. Not only is there *discord* in their lives. Not only is there *difficulty.* Not only is there certain *death.* Added to these curses there is now a fundamental *dislocation* from the *Divine.*

Adam and Eve are alone. Their souls are adrift. Their skies, so recently clear and blue, are now dark. The light has been taken from them. And thus we come to Genesis' explanation for our own sense of aloneness in the world. This is why we feel alone. It is because we have become disconnected from God.

Horace said, "They change their sky but not their soul who cross the ocean."[17] And in those steps from the garden, Adam and Eve travel the distance of an ocean. They depart from the presence of God. They enter the darkness, and now all is silent. The once pleasant and reassuring voice of God is hushed. The world is no longer a holy place, a sentiment echoed by writer Annie Dillard:

> Now the whole world seems not-holy. We have drained the light from the boughs in the sacred grove and snuffed it in the high places and along the banks of sacred streams. . . . Silence is not our heritage but our destiny; we live where we want to live. [18]

And so, we have come to the end of Genesis 3:14-24. If this were all there is to the Genesis story, there would be no hope. We would be relegated to absolute aloneness and utter chaos; to discord and destruction; and to total, complete, and everlasting loss. Let's be honest—no one wants to fall in love with a God who only looks upon this world and curses it.

Yet, according to at least one tradition, there is more to the Genesis story. There are also words of hope in this text that will mitigate God's frightening anger toward us. This hope will be the subject of our next chapter.

What we have seen in this chapter, however, is this: Who can deny that Genesis gives a horrifying but plausible answer to why things are the way they are? The Bible gives us not merely a depiction of what the world is like, but also a reason for why it is as it is: *It is this way because of our sin!*

Our traditions, on the other hand, offer us something less. No wonder Malcolm Muggeridge, when he grew old, abandoned the naive traditions of the preceding generations. He renounced the religion of this age. He abandoned the utopian tradition with its ideas of an earthly paradise and a New Jerusalem. And what did he put in its place? The worldview of Genesis. Young Malcolm grew up. He made the difficult choices men and women must make. Malcolm Muggeridge embraced Christianity. One might say he regained another kind of paradise, in the person of Jesus.

"And I will put enmity
between you and the woman,
and between your offspring and hers;
he will crush your head,
and you will strike his heel."

—GENESIS 3:15

9

REGAINING PARADISE?

I s there any hope for the human race? John Milton closes
Paradise Lost with the arresting image of Adam and Eve exit-
ing the garden. He writes:

> Some natural tears they dropped, but wiped them soon;
> The world was all before them, where to choose
> Their place of rest, and Providence their guide,
> They, hand in hand, with wandering steps and slow,
> Through Eden took their solitary way.[1]

Perhaps the most penetrating phrase in Milton's last movement is the surprising line "and Providence their guide." Milton
hints that God will continue to provide for fallen humanity —
those who now dwell east of Eden. While Adam and Eve may
be banished from the garden, forced out into the darkness and
separated from their Creator, Providence will guide them still.
They are not destitute of care. God has not utterly abandoned
them. His voice, as it were, is still with them. For Milton, *God's
curses are attended by God's graces.*[2] If this is true, what a relief! If
the God of Genesis is to be loved by us, then God must be a God
of grace as well as of judgment. For no one wants to fall in love
with a God who only curses his creation. As we mentioned in the
opening chapter of this book, within us all there is the hope that
God really does care about the events of human history.

So, did the great seventeenth-century English bard speak

wishfully on this point? Is there some evidence within Genesis 3 that warrants such a hope? As a thoughtful reader you need to ask, "Am I drinking the provisions of God from the chalice of Milton or from the fountain of Genesis? Do the Scriptures teach—as Milton hinted—that God mixes his graces with the draught of his curses?" What wonderful news if such a tradition were true! Indeed, what *good news:* "and Providence their guide . . ."

And so we ask: Are there graces of God anywhere to be found in Genesis 3 that would grant hope to the human race?

THE GRACE OF GOD IN GENESIS 3

When we look closely at Scripture, it becomes apparent that Milton's surprising phrase does have biblical support. Humanity has not been cut loose on an ocean of despair. The Bible teaches otherwise. The third chapter of Genesis, in fact, contains at least three examples of God's grace amid humanity's darkest hour.

God's Grace at the Time of the First Sin

First, the gracious activity of God is apparent *at the time of the first sin.* If Genesis 3:6, where Adam and Eve eat the forbidden fruit, is the saddest verse in the Bible, then the ninth verse of the same chapter is one of the most hopeful, because it imparts happy news for mankind. It speaks of a divine intention to impart grace to the man and the woman:

> But the LORD God called to the man, "Where are you?"

The Lord of the heavens and the earth is under no obligation to seek out mankind. But this is exactly what God does, because the God of Genesis is gracious. At the time of the fall, God takes the initiative. In the very hour of judgment God demonstrates grace. *God pursues humanity.*

God's Grace in the Judgments Themselves

It may seem odd for us to assert that grace comes through judgment, but this is precisely what Genesis 3 shows. The grace of God is seen *in* his judgments. Perhaps the words of Simone Weil, a woman well-acquainted with affliction, say it best: "[A]ffliction is the surest sign that God wishes to be loved by us; it is the most precious evidence of his tenderness."[3] What we find in Genesis is that the affliction he assigns us is evidence of his tenderness.

The truth that grace is tied to affliction is something today's reader needs to ponder. Whenever you reach out to grasp a horizon that is not rightfully yours, God's affliction will limit the length of your reach in order that you might stop grasping for that which is rightfully divine, and instead extend your hands in humility to take hold of God's goodness. This is what God does in and through his judgments. God is gracious, and we know it because God judges our sinful behavior.

C. S. Lewis pointed out that, in committing the first sin, Adam and Eve wanted "to call their souls their own. They wanted some corner in the universe in which they could say to God, 'This is our business, not yours.' What they learn [in his judgments is that] there is no such corner."[4] The judgments of God on the man and the woman mercifully show them that there is no corner in the universe to which they can run in an effort to hide from God. They belong to him alone, and *in* his judgments they will learn to cry out to him who alone can lift them out of their despair.

Think of it this way: Doesn't a loving parent demonstrate grace by exercising judgment on the inappropriate behavior of a child? How twisted our world becomes when parents neglect

to discipline their children because they don't want to be judg-
mental. This kind of parent will end up cursing the child.

And how strange it is for today's reader to reject God's curses
under the false premise that a loving God would make no moral
judgments on human behavior. On the contrary, the voice of
Genesis proclaims that God is gracious to the man and the
woman precisely *because* he judges their disobedience.

God's Grace at the Time of Their Departure from the Garden

God's grace is evident at the time of the first sin and in the midst
of his judgments. Furthermore, God's grace is seen in his preparation for mankind's departure from the garden. Look at
Genesis 3:21:

> The LORD God made garments of skin for Adam and his wife
> and clothed them.

Despite God's angry response to sin, in an act of remarkable tenderness he makes garments to protect Adam and Eve from the
harsh elements of a hostile world.

Do you remember what was said in an earlier chapter about
the consequences of the first sin? The man and the woman expe-
rienced *shame*. Now, in the act of creating garments for them, God
covers not only their bodies but also their self-conscious shame.

Recall that another consequence of the first sin is *death*. Adam
and Eve are going to die. They are now of *this* world, vulnerable
to its harshness on every front. And so God graciously covers
them with garments in order to protect them from the inevitable
wounds of a world that now works against them.

Does God care about what is going on down here? From the
vantage point of Genesis 3 we say, "Yes!" The hand of God in the
world is not some pie-in-the-sky belief made up by weak-kneed
and fearful followers of a faulty tradition. It is not a delusional

crutch. The graces of God are part and parcel of the world in which we live. We are *clothed* in his graces! Our lives are attended by God's mercy.

IS THERE A PROMISE OF A GREATER GRACE?

Of course, the greatest provision God could give to those of us who dwell east of Eden is complete rescue from *divine dislocation*. If God really cared about our fallen state, would he not orchestrate our reunion with him? This is the unspoken wish behind Milton's words, "and Providence their guide." It is the hope of sins forgiven and divine anger withdrawn. Is this kind of grace mentioned in the Bible? Is there any warrant for such a measure of eternal comfort and hope? Despite his prerogative to judge us, is God rescuing a fallen world?

Biblical Christianity claims just that. In fact, Christianity holds that Genesis 3:15 anticipates a divine design to bestow unending grace upon fallen humanity. For this text of Scripture points to nothing less than the good news of "paradise regained." We might *wish* such grace were true—but wishing does not necessarily make it so. We must focus our attention on the biblical text with all intellectual integrity and humility.

The First Good News?

The strange words of Genesis 3:15 are of central significance to biblical theology. The verse reads:

> And I will put enmity between you and the woman, and between your offspring and hers; he will crush your head, and you will strike his heel.

Christians call this verse the *protoevangelium*—that is, the "first good news." The expression "good news" is a free translation of the Greek word for "gospel." The message of the Christian gospel is that the death and resurrection of Jesus crushed the head of Satan — who, as we shall see shortly, is personified in the serpent of Genesis 3.

According to New Testament writings, Jesus is the "off-spring" foreshadowed in Genesis 3:15. He is the one who brings about the great reversal of mankind's plunge into sin and destruction. Jesus overcomes the curse of God upon humanity by defeating death and sin on our behalf. Therefore, according to biblical Christianity, Genesis 3:15 points to God's promise to rescue humanity from its divine dislocation.

With this in mind, it is reasonable — and important — to ask a question of the Christian tradition: "On what basis do you believe that the good news of paradise regained is anticipated in this verse?" In other words, is this truly the first good news after mankind's fall into sin? Whether Genesis 3:15 is, in fact, the first good news depends upon how we answer two additional questions:

- Does God's curse on the serpent apply to Satan, who is the "evil one" of Scripture?

- Does the offspring of the woman refer to Jesus of Nazareth?

In the next two sections we will explain why Christians believe the serpent to be Satan and the offspring or "seed"[5] to be Jesus.

The Serpent and Satan

The basis for Christian hope stems from an understanding 1) that the Bible has a unified message, and, 2) that the message of Genesis is only the first part of the message of the entire Bible. We affirm that Genesis complements the teaching of the New

Testament. Moreover, it is clear that the New Testament unmasks the serpent of Genesis 3 as Satan.

The most striking proof-text for these assertions takes the reader from the first book of the Bible to the last—the apocalyptic book of Revelation. In the twelfth chapter of Revelation we find a description of an altercation between a woman and a dragon—imagery strikingly similar to that of Genesis 3. In Revelation 12:9 we find the explicit connection between the dragon, the serpent of Genesis 3, and Satan:

> The great dragon was hurled down—that ancient serpent called the devil or Satan, who leads the whole world astray. He was hurled to the earth, and his angels with him.

It is clear that the writer of Revelation identifies the dragon not only with Satan (or the devil) but also with "that ancient serpent" of Genesis 3:15. It is to this early text of Scripture that the writer looks back. The wily serpent of Genesis 3 is also the deadly dragon of Revelation 12—and both are none other than Satan personified.

The Seed and the Savior

Christianity holds that the seed of the woman who crushes the head of the serpent (Satan) is Jesus of Nazareth. How so? Well, interestingly, in the translation of Genesis 3:15, we find that God's promise refers to a single person. The phrase is, *"he* will crush your head." The Gospel writer Luke, by tracing the genealogy of Jesus back to the seed of Adam and Eve (Luke 3:23-38), is making the point that Jesus is the "he" of Genesis 3:15. He, Jesus, is the promised seed.

The concept of a victorious seed in Genesis 3 figures prominently in the rest of Scripture. Abraham is told that all peoples will be blessed through his seed (Genesis 12 and 15). Later, the apostle Paul makes a direct link between Jesus Christ and the fulfillment of God's "seed promise" to Abraham. In Galatians 3:16 (emphasis added) Paul writes:

> The Scripture does not say, "and to seeds," meaning many people, but "and to your seed," meaning one person, *who is Christ.*

Thus, Christians believe Jesus Christ to be hinted at in Genesis 3:15. He, Jesus, is both seed and Savior.

GRAPPLING WITH THE GOSPEL IN GENESIS

The Voice of Our Traditions

Certainly you don't need reminding that most traditions completely reject and dismiss the above interpretation of the seed and the serpent. Many people, past and present, contend that the Bible is not a coherent whole—that it does not have a unified message. They argue that what goes on in Revelation has nothing to do with what is said in Genesis. The serpent is not Satan. Furthermore, these traditions reject the notion that Jesus is the intended seed. Jesus, they say, is not the thread that runs from the beginning to the end of Scripture.

The influential Old Testament scholar Hermann Gunkel, who lived at the turn of the last century, disbelieved the connection between the serpent imagery in Genesis and the Satan of Revelation. Of Genesis 3:15 he writes: "The saying suggests quite distinctly that, for the narrator, the serpent is an animal and nothing more." Gunkel goes on to quote another writer: "The devil does not crawl on his belly and eat dust." Continuing his line of argument, he even rejects the idea that the serpent is a real serpent, and he relegates the entire biblical text to

> the category of myths and fairy tales . . . which tell how certain animals came by their unusual characteristics, why the

flounder has its oblique mouth, the donkey his long ears, and the bear its stumpy tail.[6]

Traditions Collide

So there you have it in a nutshell—two diametrically opposed ways to read and interpret Genesis 3:15. For Christianity, this verse points to a promise of good news, of hope for the human race, of paradise regained through the death and resurrection of Jesus Christ. For other traditions, Genesis 3:15 is better suited to be read alongside Rudyard Kipling's *Just So Stories,* such as "How the Monkey Got Its Tail." If Gunkel and his tradition are correct, then we might subtitle the account in Genesis 3 "Why the Snake Slithers on Its Belly."

FINAL THOUGHTS

We cannot tell you, the reader, what to make of the Bible. We certainly cannot convince you to embrace Christianity against your will. What we have seen is that there are two ways to read the Bible. It can be read as containing a unified message to us from God, or merely as a disparate collection of human letters assembled by various writers over the centuries—a great work of literature, perhaps, but certainly not a revelation from the God who made the universe.

The voice of Christianity contends that the Bible, taken as a whole, begins to make sense when it is read with Jesus at the center. It is not understood by haggling over what type of literature Genesis is as compared to the book of Revelation. You will never grasp the central plot line of the Bible by arguing over technicalities. Rather, you will come to know the thrust of the Bible's message by what C. S. Lewis likened to the way we know a smell or a taste. As you read further in the Bible you will discover that it smells and tastes of God rescuing humanity from the first sin.

This divine rescue in the person and work of Jesus is its motif; and it is repeated and reinforced again and again in a variety of settings from cover to cover.

Thinking people all through the centuries have come to this conclusion. Thousands upon thousands have affirmed that Jesus is the one promised to the woman in the garden so long ago. Moreover, they have confessed — sometimes at peril to their lives — that Jesus is the one who, in his death and resurrection, crushed the head of the serpent, Satan, thus defeating his evil hold on humankind.

Lebanese scholar and educator Charles Malik, who served for a time as president of the United Nations General Assembly, writes,

> This is a very strange situation — that one brought up in Galilee some two thousand years ago should be the clue to the being and order of the universe, the way out of self-entanglement. Let us not be poetic or sentimental, or fall into all sorts of idealistic-metaphysical interpretations. Above all, let us not demythologize. What is here affirmed, what the church affirms . . . is that a man born near Jerusalem and crucified just outside the city wall is literally, truly, himself, and none other, the answer not only to the question of the origin and order of the universe but for all those who are lost in the wilderness of existence, those who worship wealth or acclaim or power or country or culture, who worship mind or art or spouse or children or scientific theory or political cause or anything you can name, and who thereby proceed unwittingly on the path of corruption.[7]

Malik's words are worth repeating: "Jesus . . . is . . . the answer not only to the question of the origin and order of the universe but for all those who are lost in the wilderness of existence."

Jesus — the answer to life's big questions?

[44]*[Jesus] said to them, "This is what I told you while I was still with you: Everything must be fulfilled that is written about me in the Law of Moses, the Prophets and the Psalms."*

[45]*Then he opened their minds so they could understand the Scriptures.* [46]*He told them, "This is what is written: The Christ will suffer and rise from the dead on the third day,* [47]*and repentance and forgiveness of sins will be preached in his name to all nations, beginning at Jerusalem."*

—LUKE 24:44-47

10

THE INESCAPABLE ISSUE

W e come now to the end of this book — but not the end of
the conversation. In fact, your great conversation with
the Christian faith may be only just beginning. Winston
Churchill, in another context, said:

> Now is not the end. It is not even the beginning of the end. But
> it is, perhaps, the end of the beginning.[1]

So we stand together at the end of the beginning. And having
"finished the beginning," one might wonder, "How do I proceed
to the end?"

We suggest that the answer might lie in further conversation
with the Bible. You must wrestle now with questions like those
raised by Leo Strauss, whom we heard from in chapter 1:

> Is the Bible the work of the human mind? Is it not the work of
> God?[2]

An intriguing thought is that the entire Bible might be nothing less than the voice of God. This may be the next big question that the reader needs to answer: "Is the Bible the work of
God?"

We should tell you that in the recent past Christians have
sought to assist you in answering this question in a variety of
ways. One such approach is "evidentialism." By amassing evi-

dence and data to substantiate that the Bible is without errors or contradictions, evidentialists felt that you would be convinced that the Bible is not the work of the human mind but unquestionably the Word of God.

We, however, would put forward a different starting point. We encourage you to ask one simple question: *Is there a unifying message to the Bible?* Read the Bible in its entirety. Discern its overall message. Understand how its various parts relate to that message. Then you will be ready to conclude whether or not it is the work of God.

In the process, inevitably you will engage Jesus in conversation. For, in the end, all questions on the unity of the Bible must confront the person of Jesus. You must decide if Jesus is the unifying figure on the pages of Scripture. For thoughtful Bible readers, confronting Jesus of Nazareth is unavoidable. Gerhard von Rad has put the inescapable issue this way:

> All exegesis of the Old Testament depends on whom one thinks Jesus Christ to be.[3]

Interestingly, Luke's Gospel finds Jesus making a remarkable claim: "Everything must be fulfilled that is written about me in the Law of Moses, the Prophets and the Psalms" (Luke 24:44). And in the Gospel of John, Jesus says, "If you believed Moses, you would believe me, for he wrote about me" (John 5:46). In the end, all your big questions will require a conclusion regarding who you think Jesus is.

But be warned: The Bible is a surprising book. It may become more to you than something you read—you may find that by reading it you encounter "the Genesis Factor"—the viable but often overlooked voice of God. Flannery O'Connor has written a trenchant narrative depicting just such an unexpected belief. It is an interchange between Sheppard, a social worker, and Johnson, the man he is trying to help:

"What's that you're reading?" Sheppard asked, sitting down. "The Holy Bible," Johnson said.

Sheppard leaned forward and said in a low furious voice, "Put that Bible up . . . and eat your dinner. . . ."

The boy stopped and looked up. His expression was startled but pleased.

"That book is something for you to hide behind," Sheppard said. "It's for cowards, people who are afraid to stand on their own feet and figure things out for themselves. . . ."

Sheppard reached across the table to grab the book but Johnson snatched it and put it in his lap.

Sheppard laughed. "You don't believe in that book and you know you don't believe in it!"

"I believe it!" Johnson said. "You don't know what I believe and what I don't."

Sheppard shook his head. "You don't believe it. You're too intelligent."

"I ain't too intelligent," the boy muttered. "You don't know nothing about me. Even if I didn't believe it, it would still be true."

"You don't believe it!" Sheppard said. His face was taut.

"I believe it!" Johnson said breathlessly. "I'll show you I believe it!" He opened the book in his lap and tore out a page of it and thrust it into his mouth. His jaws worked furiously and the paper crackled as he chewed it.

"Stop this," Sheppard said in a dry, burnt-out voice. "Stop it."

The boy raised the Bible and tore out a page with his teeth and began grinding it in his mouth, his eyes burning.

Sheppard reached across the table and knocked the book out of his hand. "Leave the table," he said coldly.

Johnson swallowed what was in his mouth. His eyes widened as if a vision of splendor were opening up before him. "I've eaten it!" he breathed. "I've eaten it like Ezekiel and it was honey to my mouth!"

"Leave this table," Sheppard said. His hands were clenched beside his plate.

"I've eaten it!" the boy cried. Wonder transformed his face. "I've eaten it like Ezekiel and I don't want none of your food after it nor no more ever more."[4]

NOTES

Preface

1. Leo Tolstoy, *Anna Karenina* (New York: Bantam, 1981) pp. 470-471.
2. J. Gresham Machen, *Christianity and Liberalism* (Grand Rapids, Mich.: Eerdmans, 1923), p. 1.
3. C. S. Lewis, *Mere Christianity* (New York: Macmillan, 1952), p. 6.

Chapter 1 – A Conversation Starter

1. Foreword to Stephen Hawking, *A Brief History of Time,* tenth anniversary edition (New York: Bantam, 1998), p. vii.
2. Ibid.
3. Quoted in Alvin Plantinga, "On Christian Scholarship," in Theodore M. Hesburgh, ed., *The Challenge and Promise of a Catholic University* (South Bend, Ind.: Notre Dame University Press, 1994), p. 269. Plantinga gives a succinct summary of modern worldviews, which we refer to as "traditions" or "voices" in this book.
4. "In the Beginning: God and Science," *Time* (February 5, 1979), p. 149.
5. For a more detailed argument, see "What Can We Know? The Dialogue with Science," chapter 4 of Lesslie Newbigin, *Foolishness to the Greeks* (Grand Rapids, Mich.: Eerdmans, 1986), pp. 65-94.
6. David F. Wells, *No Place for Truth* (Grand Rapids, Mich.: Eerdmans, 1993), p. 263.
7. J. D. Salinger, "Teddy," in *Nine Stories* (Boston: Little, Brown, 1953), p. 288.
8. Shirley MacLaine, *Dancing in the Light* (New York: Bantam, 1986), p. 358.
9. See *The New International Dictionary of the Christian Church,* ed. J. D. Douglas (Grand Rapids, Mich.: Zondervan, 1974), p. 745.
10. Plantinga labels this tradition, which we are calling pervasive supernaturalism, as 'creative anti-realism'. His emphasis is on the creative aspect of this worldview. From a typed manuscript copy of the chapter, p. 10.
11. Leo Strauss, in a lecture given in the "Works of the Mind" series at University College, University of Chicago, January 25, 1957.

12. This selection of worldviews or traditions is by no means exhaustive, but merely representative. We could just as easily have added ten others, including the various world religions such as Judaism, Islam, Catholicism, and the many variants of Protestantism.

13. Attributed to Torrance; personal communication.

Chapter 2 – A View of the Stars

1. Macro-evolution is the idea that, given time, one might observe an organism change from one species into a completely new species. Micro-evolution is the idea that, given time, one might observe change within a particular species.

2. Mortimer Adler, *How to Read a Book* (New York: Simon & Schuster, 1972), pp. 46-47. In chapter 5, "How to Be a Demanding Reader," Adler claims that there are four questions to ask of any book: 1) What is the book about as a whole? 2) What is being said in detail and how? 3) Is the book true, in whole or in part? 4) What of it? Adler further argues that "the art of reading on any level above the elementary consists in the habit of *asking the right questions in the right order"* (emphasis added).

3. We, as the authors, want to clarify three assumptions we have about reading Genesis on its own terms.

    An Original Context. Our first assumption is that we ought to read Genesis with the original context in mind. We would argue that Genesis was written to a *particular people* at a *particular time*. The natural tendency is to read with a priority on contemporary relevance. Since conversations on origins are prevalent today, we often ask such questions of Genesis. But if we consider that the writer may be addressing a different set of questions, it might keep us from posing too quickly our particular questions of the text. This is our first assumption: that Genesis was originally written to ancient Israel, not to us.

    A Unified Whole. Our second assumption is that we ought to read Genesis as a complete book. (In our book, we will look primarily at the first three chapters of Genesis, but will seek to do so with the entire book in view.) Unfortunately, our traditions often dictate otherwise. Our present inability to think about Genesis as a unified whole stems, in part, from a tendency to read according to the "JEDP" or "documentary hypothesis" tradition. As you may know, this theory divides the Mosaic writings according to hypothetical sources. It puts forth the idea that Moses was not the sole author or editor of Genesis and the other books of the Pentateuch. (JEDP is the common abbreviation for four so-called literary sources postulated by German scholars as lying behind the Pentateuch and possibly later Old Testament books. "J" is derived from *Jahwe*, German for Yahweh or Jehovah—a Hebrew name for God. "E" is from Elohim—another Hebrew name for God. "D" is from Deuteronomy; and "P" is from Pentateuch. For a brief summary of each source, see Bruce M. Metzger and Michael D. Coogan, eds., *The Oxford Companion to the Bible* [New York: Oxford University Press, 1993]: p. 338 for the "J" source; p. 173 for "E"; p. 567 for "P"; and p. 147 for "D".)

The JEDP tradition (whether or not it is correct) overlooks the fact that Genesis *is* a book. No wonder the highly reputable Jewish scholar Nahum Sarna said of this tradition, "Whatever the merits or demerits of this type of analysis, beyond doubt the book of Genesis came down to us not as a composite of disparate elements, but as a unified document with a life, coherence, and integrity of its own. For this reason a fragmentary approach to it cannot provide an adequate understanding of the whole" [Nahum Sarna, *The JPS Torah Commentary: Genesis* (Philadelphia: Jewish Publication Society, 1989), p. xvi). Later, Sarna calls the methodology of JEDP "a coroner's approach . . . [like] dissecting a literary corpse" (ibid.). Sarna encourages all of us to read Genesis as one would read any other book, by first asking Adler's question: "What is the book about as a whole?"

A Historical Record. Third, we assume that Genesis presents itself as a historical record of one kind or another. Now, obviously, no one was present at the beginning of creation. Some argue that Genesis, therefore, is not a historical record. And according to today's rules for writing history, we would agree. Only a fool would argue that someone was there at the beginning, recording the events set before us in Genesis 1. Genesis is not a history of origins *in that sense*. Nevertheless, in our minds, the writer seems concerned to root the history of Israel's family tree in the soil of universal beginnings. In fact, the opening chapters of Genesis include three genealogies (Adam, chapter 5; Noah's sons, chapter 10; Shem to Abram, chapter 11). Each genealogy serves to connect Abraham and the patriarchs to Adam and the beginnings of history. (There are two additional places in the first eleven chapters where the Hebrew word *toledot*, which introduces the genealogies, is used: in Genesis 2:4, of the heavens and the earth; and in Genesis 5:9, of Noah.) In this sense the first chapter of Genesis *is* a historical record.

We agree with the conclusion of twentieth-century theologian Francis Schaeffer, who wrote "The mentality of the whole Scripture is that creation is as historically real as the history of the Jews and our present moment of time. Both the Old and the New Testaments deliberately root themselves back in the early chapters of Genesis, insisting that they are a record of historical events" (Francis Schaeffer, *Genesis in Space and Time,* book one in *The Complete Works of Francis Schaeffer, Volume Two: A Christian View of the Bible as Truth* [Wheaton, Ill.: Crossway, 1982], p. 7).

These are our assumptions. When we read Genesis for answers to life's universal questions, we try to read it in its original context, as a unified book, and as a historical document. Without these assumptions we might miss Adler's advice and raise a set of questions overly focused on contemporary relevance.

Adler's suggestion hems us in. It sets our particular questions aside so that we are free to ask the single most important question: What is Genesis about as a whole?

4. Our English translations disguise some of the grammatical complexities of the Hebrew text. In Hebrew, Genesis 1:1 opens with the word *b-reshit.* This word is comprised of two parts: first, the preposition *b-,* which means "in"; and, second, *reshit,* which means "beginnings." The New International Version translates it: "In the beginning." Strictly speaking, though, the Hebrew term stands alone, without a definite article: "In beginning."

The implications of this are: verse 1 may *not* be the main clause. The writer may be articulating *traditional dualism.* Thus, instead of,

In *the* beginning God created the heavens and the earth . . .

we would have,

When God did this ("created," verse 1), the earth *was already, and independent from him,* like that ("formless and empty," verse 2).

According to traditional dualism, Genesis teaches neither theism nor naturalism, but that both God and matter coexist in eternity. However, when we read Genesis within the context of the Torah, it is clear that the writer rejects traditional dualism.

There is another tradition, however, which while rejecting traditional dualism does argue for the eternality of matter along different lines. We call this *sophisticated dualism.* Highly respected thinkers such as Philo and committed Christians such as John Milton fall within this tradition. To summarize this approach we show the following interpretation:

Verse 1: God exists in the beginning.

Verse 2: Matter exists eternally *within* God.

Verse 3: A preexistent God creates from preexistent matter, which is somehow dependent on him.

In a recent television commercial for a sports beverage, athletes are shown performing at their creative best. Michael Jordan takes a drink and makes a heroic shot. The question "*Is it in you?*" appears on the screen. For the sophisticated dualist, the creative activity of God in Genesis 1 is possible only because *matter was and always will be within God.* Creation, according to this view, is the result of God speaking into existence what—up to that point—had been eternally concealed *within* his person. For the sophisticated dualist, God's creative flourish is much greater than any human feat, because God was never in need of "drinking in" matter; rather, the eternality of matter was from all time preexistent within him.

There are grammatical options, however, that may lead one away from sophisticated dualism and the eternality of matter. Instead of a period at the end of verse 1, the translators could have used a *semicolon.* We say this because the very first word in the Hebrew text of verse 2 is the conjunction *va,* or "and." Conjunctions are "joiners," which indicate some connection or relationship to what has just been said. According to this view, *the author intends to join together verses 1 and 2.*

On the basis of this connection, Genesis 1:1 *may very well* contain the *real* creative activity of God. To paraphrase as simply as possible, this third view on origins is that,

1:1 "In the beginning God created the heavens and the earth (*out of nothing*);

1:2 "And the earth, *immediately after he created it out of nothing,* was without form—it was uninhabitable—it was a dark and watery mass—and the Spirit of God was hovering over it in anticipation.

1:3 "Then God said, 'Let there be light' . . ."

5. Richard Dawkins, *The Blind Watchmaker: Why the Evidence of Evolution Reveals a Universe without Design* (New York: W. W. Norton, 1996), p. 316.

6. Quoted in Vernard Eller, *The Simple Life* (Grand Rapids, Mich.: Eerdmans, 1973), p. 12.

Chapter 3 – The Six-Day Song

1. See C. S. Lewis, *The Magician's Nephew*, Chronicles of Narnia (New York: Collier, 1955), p. 116.

2. The words "formless and empty" together form a "hendiadys" — that is, two words that have one meaning (like "spic and span" or "hem and haw"). In Genesis 1:2 the Hebrew words for "formless" and "empty," taken together, form the lyrical rhyming phrase *tohu wabohu*.

3. The following chart summarizes this correspondence:

GOD'S WORKDAYS

Days 1-3 *Forming*			Days 4-6 *Filling*		
Day 1	1:3-5	*Light*	Day 4	1:14-19	*Lights*
Day 2	1:6-8	*Water and Sky*	Day 5	1:20-23	*Water and Sky*
Day 3	1:9-13	*Earth*	Day 6	1:24-31	*Earth*
Day 7	*God's Rest*				

4. See *The New International Dictionary of the Christian Church*, ed. J. D. Douglas (Grand Rapids, Mich.: Zondervan, 1974), p. 1005.

5. Arthur Conan Doyle, "The Naval Treaty," in *Sherlock Holmes: The Complete Novels and Stories*, vol. 1 (New York: Bantam, 1986), p. 624.

Chapter 4 – The Surprise of Seven

1. As quoted in Iain Murray and D. Martyn Lloyd Jones, *The Fight of Faith 1939-1981* (Carlisle, Pa.: The Banner of Truth Trust, 1990), p. 57.

2. The point here has less to do with how long the days lasted in Genesis than with the stunning accomplishment it would have been for any God to create everything, out of nothing, by the power of his word. Our view on the length of the days will be explained later in this chapter.

3. The voice of the prophets echo this truth as well. Isaiah says, "Do you not know? Have you not heard? The LORD is the everlasting God, *the Creator* of the ends of the earth. *He will not grow tired or weary*" (40:28, emphasis added). No, according to the voice of Genesis and the whole Bible, God does not rest because he is fatigued or disengaged.

4. Because this illustration relates specifically to one of us, we are using the first-person-singular pronoun.

5. Luke 6:1-10 and John 5:1-17 are representative of the many Gospel texts that record Jesus' views on the Sabbath.

6. C. John Collins, "Reading Genesis 1:1–2:3 as an Act of Communication: Discourse Analysis and Literal Interpretation," unpublished manuscript, p. 5.

7. In contrast to an anthropomorphism, in which human traits are attributed to God, the writer of Genesis uses a theomorphism: It is we who are like God. We, who are created in God's image, rest because God rests.

8. The idea is not unlike Plato's analogy of the cave. The person who sees only shadows on the wall of the cave, but not the reality itself, will consider the shadows themselves to be the reality. But the shadows, in actuality, are merely projected from what is real.

9. See C. S. Lewis, "Pilgrim's Regress," in *The Collected Works of C. S. Lewis* (New York: Inspirational Press, 1996), p. 49.

10. Graeme Goldsworthy, *Gospel and Kingdom: A Christian Interpretation of the Old Testament* (Carlisle, England: Paternoster, 1996).

Chapter 5 – Mud as Man

1. For thoughtful readers, the words of 2:4 ("This is the account . . .") may provoke the following questions: "Is the author now going to follow up the creation narrative of chapter 1 with a second and differing account in chapter 2?" And, "If so, are the first two chapters of the Bible giving separate and competing views of creation?" Many today would also ask, "Must we read these two accounts as if they were written by one and the same author? Or, might it not be better to assume that the wordings of 1:1 and 2:4, different as they are, demonstrate the reality of divergent sources regarding creation accounts?"

   At the outset you should know that questions like these are quite natural and in fact are not new. Regardless of where you land on issues of multiple authorship of Genesis, we believe that one question can be answered with great certainty: The creation accounts of Genesis 1 and 2 are not competing with each other. We concur with Nahum Sarna, who said, "Chapter 2 is not another creation story. As such it would be singularly incomplete. In fact, it presupposes a knowledge of much of the preceding account of Genesis" (*The JPS Torah Commentary: Genesis* [Philadelphia: The Jewish Publication Society, 1989], p. 16).

2. Because this illustration relates specifically to one of us, we are using the first-person-singular pronoun.

3. Evidently God created the first man prior to the first woman. We know from 1:26-27 that both were created in the image of God. Therefore, while some of the following comments come from the text that refers solely to the creation of the first man, we will apply its teaching inclusively to both men and women.

4. Quoted in Francis Darwin, *Life and Letters of Charles Darwin*, vol. 2 (New York: Appleton, 1896), p. 703. The letter was written in 1871.

5. Kurt Vonnegut, Jr., *Cat's Cradle* (New York: Dell, 1970), p. 177. Vonnegut is quoted in James W. Sire, *The Universe Next Door* (Downers Grove, Ill.: InterVarsity Press, 1976). We highly recommend Sire's book to readers who want a more in-depth exploraion of worldviews.

6. Quoted in Martin Gardiner, *The Flight of Peter Fromm* (Amherst, N.Y.: Prometheus, 1994), pp. 28-29.

7. Quoted in Alvin Plantinga, "On Christian Scholarship," in Theodore M. Hesburgh, ed., *The Challenge and Promise of a Catholic University* (South Bend, Ind.: Notre Dame University Press, 1994), p. 276.

8. Bob Dylan, "Man Gave Names to All the Animals," as recorded on the album *Slow Train Coming* (Columbia, Special Rider Music, 1979).

9. From an advertisement in *Parade* magazine, March 14, 1999, p. 12.

10. The Bible affirms equally the estate of marriage and the estate of singleness. For the affirmation of marriage, see Genesis 1:27-28 and Proverbs 18:22; for the affirmation of singleness, see 1 Corinthians 7:7-8, 32-34.

Chapter 6 – The Intoxicating Program

1. As quoted in Gerhard von Rad, *Genesis* (Philadelphia: Westminster, 1961), p. 86.

2. Our approach to Genesis lies within the scope of biblical theology as summarized by Graeme Goldsworthy in *According to Plan: The Unfolding Revelation of God in the Bible* (Leicester, England: InterVarsity, 1991). See especially chapters 1–7 (pp. 19-103). We highly recommend this book to anyone who is grappling with the early chapters of Genesis.

3. C. S. Lewis, *The Allegory of Love* (London: Oxford University Press, 1938), p. 225.

4. Paul Johnson, *The Quest for God: A Personal Pilgrimage* (New York: HarperCollins, 1996), p. 61.

5. Quoted by Dorothy Sayers in her preface to G. K. Chesterton, *The Surprise* (New York: Sheed & Ward, 1953), p. 8

6. Cited in previous note.

7. Dietrich Bonhoeffer, *Temptation* (London: SCM, 1961), p. 33.

8. Derek Kidner, *Genesis: An Introduction and Commentary* (Downers Grove, Ill.: InterVarsity Press, 1967), p. 68.

Chapter 7 – A Sense of Estrangement

1. Friedrich Nietzsche, *Beyond Good and Evil* (London: Penguin, 1990).

2. The argument of Romans (see Rom. 5:12-14) confirms that God held Adam responsible for the first sin.

3. Jonathan Edwards, *The Works of Jonathan Edwards,* vol. 1 (Carlisle, Pa.: Banner of Truth, 1986), p. 181.

4. Martin Gardner, *The Flight of Peter Fromm* (Amherst, N.Y.: Prometheus, 1994), pp. 169-170.

5. Blaise Pascal, *Pensées* (New York: Oxford University Press, 1995), p. 42.

Chapter 8 – Utopian Dreams

1. Malcolm Muggeridge, *Jesus Rediscovered* (Glasgow: Collins, 1985), p. 15.

2. John Milton, "Paradise Lost," in *The Complete Poems of John Milton,* Harvard Classics (New York: P. F. Collier, 1937), p. 308.

3. What does the strange-sounding judgment of verse 16 mean? The pairing of the Hebrew words for "desire" and "rule" appear in only two other texts in all of Scripture, once in Song of Songs (chapter 7) and the other time in Genesis 4. Studying the writer's use of these two words in Genesis 4 helps us to understand their meaning in our own text. In Genesis 4 Cain has offered a sacrifice that is unacceptable to God. In response, God says to Cain, " . . . but if you do not do what is right, sin is crouching at your door. It desires to have you, but you must master it" (v. 7). The words "desires" and "master" are the very ones used in God's judgment on the woman. In the case of Cain, they obviously mean that sin desires to rule over him, but he must rule over it. Returning, then, to the strange judgment on the woman, we see that Eve will now have a desire to rule over her husband, but it is he who will master her in ungodly ways. There will be great dispute between man and woman—discord and fighting will enter a relationship that was once complementary and harmonious.

4. Quoted in Paul Johnson, *Intellectuals* (New York: Harper & Row, 1988), p. 201, punctuation and emphasis added.

5. Ibid., pp. 218-219.

6. Ibid., p. 235.

7. Exact source unknown.

8. Quoted in R. Kent Hughes, *Disciplines of a Godly Man* (Wheaton, Ill.: Crossway, 1991), p. 139.

9. Simone Weil, *Gateway to God*, ed. David Raper (London: Fontana, 1975.), pp. 55-56.

10. Quoted in Ernest T. Campbell, *Locked in a Room with Open Doors* (Waco, Tex.: Word, 1974), p. 117.

11. Undoubtedly, some of our readers find work highly enjoyable, which may seem to be at odds with the Bible's teaching on the curse. However, one should remember that the Bible also teaches that work had a divine dignity prior to the Fall (Genesis 2:15: "The LORD God took the man and put him in the Garden of Eden to work it and take care of it."). Significant traces of this positive aspect of work remain, even after the fall.

12. Quoted in a work by A. W. Pink (exact reference unknown).

13. Albert Camus, *The Plague*, trans. Stuart Gilbert (New York: Random House, 1948), p. 278.

14. As quoted in Kenneth E. Kirk, *The Vision of God*, abridged edition (Harrisburg, Pa.: Morehouse, 1991), p. 14.

15. John Milton, "Paradise Lost," in *The Complete Poems of John Milton*, Harvard Classics (New York: P. F. Collier, 1937), pp. 325-326.

16. Flannery O'Conner had some sense of this divine protectiveness when she wrote of her Southern roots, "The south is traditionally hostile to outsiders except on her own terms. She is traditionally against intruders, foreigners from Chicago or New Jersey, all those who come from afar with moral energy that increases in direct proportion to their distance from home" (Flannery O'Connor, "The Catholic Novelist in the Protestant South," in *Flannery O'Connor: Collected Works* [New York: Library of America, 1988], p. 856).

17. Quoted in Thomas Cahill, *How the Irish Saved Civilization* (New York: Doubleday, 1995), p. 193.

18. Annie Dillard, *Teaching a Stone to Talk* (New York: Harper & Row, 1982), p. 69.

Chapter 9 — Regaining Paradise?

1. John Milton, "Paradise Lost," in *The Complete Poems of John Milton*, Harvard Classics (New York: P. F. Collier, 1937), p. 358.

2. Precisely how much meaning the reader can assume from Milton's use of the term "Providence" is debated by some. See Thomas N. Corns, *Regaining Paradise Lost* (White Plains, N.Y.: Longman, 1994), pp. 10-11.

3. Simone Weil, *On Science, Necessity, and the Love of God,* trans. Richard Rees (London: Oxford University Press, 1968), p.193.

4. Quoted in *The Quotable Lewis* (Carol Stream, Ill.: Tyndale, 1989), p. 213.

5. Where the New International Version of the Bible in Genesis 3:15 says "offspring," many other Bible versions use the word "seed." In Galatians 3:16, which we will look at next, the NIV also uses "seed." The two words mean essentially the same thing.

6. Hermann Gunkel, *Genesis* (Macon, Ga.: Mercer University Press, 1997), see pp. 20-21.

7. Charles Malik, in Kelly Monroe, ed., *Finding God at Harvard: Spiritual Journeys of Thinking Christians* (Grand Rapids, Mich.: Zondervan, 1996), p. 342.

Chapter 10 – The Inescapable Issue

1. Quoted in Charles Eade, ed., *The End of the Beginning: War Speeches by the Right Honorable Winston S. Churchill* (Boston: Little, Brown, 1943), p. 214.

2. Leo Strauss, in a lecture given in the "Works of the Mind" series at University College, University of Chicago, January 25, 1957.

3. Gerhard von Rad, *Genesis* (Philadelphia: Westminster, 1961), p. 41.

4. Flannery O'Connor, "The Lame Shall Enter First," in *Flannery O'Connor: Collected Works* (New York: Library of America, 1988), pp. 626-628.